new japanese cuisine

Shunju new japanese cuisine

foreword by Charlie Trotter

text and recipes by
Takashi Sugimoto
and Marcia Iwatate

photography by
Masano Kawana

food preparation and styling by
Marcia Iwatate and the Shunju chefs

PERIPLUS

Published by Periplus Editions
with editorial offices at
130 Joo Seng Road #06-01
Singapore 368357

Distributed by
North America
Tuttle Publishing
364 Innovation Drive
North Clarendon
VT 05759-9436, USA
Tel (802) 773-8930; fax (802) 773-6993

Japan and Korea
Tuttle Publishing
Yaekari Building, 3F, 5-4-12
Osaki, Shinagawa-Ku
Tokyo 141 0032, Japan
Tel (81-3) 5437-0171; fax (81-3) 5437-0755

Asia Pacific
Berkeley Books Pte Ltd
130 Joo Seng Road #06-01
Singapore 368357
Tel (65) 6280-1330; fax (65) 6280-6290

Creative director: Christina Ong
Book design by Loretta Reilly
Design and layout consultants: Marcia Iwatate
and Toshiaki Hirai

contents

Spring is the season of new life, the beginning of a New Year in the lunar calendar. Wild vegetables peek out from the mountain soil and the most eagerly awaited is the bamboo shoot. Our recipes provide all the variations for preparing this vegetable and all other Spring delicacies.

Celebrate the arrival of summer with *ayu* (sweetfish): this section provides various recipes for this summer favorite, and for other delights of the season, including tofu and miniature eggplants.

The most representative of the autumn delicacies is the fungus family, and *matsutake*, or pine mushroom, reigns supreme. Enjoy a selection of wild mushrooms prepared in different styles, or a selection of other delectable recipes for the season, such as lamb chops broiled over charcoal or exquisite duck and scallion miso grilled on magnolia leaf.

Among the seasonal specialties are blowfish, crabs, oysters and anglerfish, all of which are served in simple, unpretentious styles. Throw a stylish dinner party with chicken meatball hotpot, with cauliflower mousse and braised *daikon* with glazed sauce, then finish it off with fragrant jellied *yuzu* (citrus fruit).

foreword

Traditional Japanese cuisine is noted for its elegant simplicity and exquisite purity of taste, method, and appearance. Here at Charlie Trotter's we have practiced and appreciated the minimalistic Japanese approach for many years — in the use of Japanese ceramics, flavorings, and even fresh fish from Japan. It was for this reason that I was so excited to learn of this new cookbook from Tokyo's pioneering restaurant group.

The Shunju restaurants created by Takashi Sugimoto and Marcia Iwatate epitomize the aesthetic of their country to such an extent that they have almost single-handedly created a revolution in Japanese cooking akin to the "new cuisine" movements that swept France, the United States, and Australia during past decades.

Like most revolutions, Shunju's is rooted in the past but looks to the future. It represents a return to the essence of Japanese cooking — beginning with a search for the finest ingredients, including freshly-caught fish, organically-grown seasonal vegetables, and free-range, hormone-free meat and poultry. It eschews processed industrial foods and the overwrought fine dining preparations that have become all too commonplace in Japan as elsewhere — in favor of a truly modern (and at the same time truly traditional) approach to dining. Back to basics but also forward to a new awareness.

The other thing I appreciate about Shunju is the superb "traditional meets modern" Japanese interiors and the emphasis on savoring a meal slowly with friends over glasses of fine *sake*, *shoju*, and herbally-infused tonics.

The recipes and photos on these pages are truly a delight for all the senses. This marvelous work will inspire amateurs and professionals alike.

Charlie Trotter

the Shunju way

"The philosophy of my design is not to design for design's sake but to seek a perception of a space, in memory and time." — Takashi Sugimoto

the shunju philosophy

Although the materials which I have installed in Shunju such as the solid walnut plank shaved with the traditional carpenter's hatchet, the sidewalk grating reclaimed from London subways, the hand-plastered mud walls, and the Korean antiques may seem to represent tradition or antiquity, they express something new to me as I perceive a continuity of time which will survive beyond our present time and lives.

I value such elements as nature and time, the textures of genuine materials, and the state of nothingness or emptiness of thought in this chaotic city of design. The philosophy of my design is not to design for design's sake but to seek a perception of a space, in memory and time.

left The "show" kitchen in our Bunkamura-dori restaurant. Counter seats are the most sought after in all our restaurants as they allow our clients to discuss that day's ingredients with our chefs and to observe their preparations. opposite The dining hall of our Toriizaka restaurant. Although all our other restaurants have table seats, this restaurant is designed with floor seating only. Clients remove their shoes before entering the dining area which is composed of three areas: counter seating, an open dining area partitioned with bamboo screens and steel gratings from the London subway, and private rooms.

history The history of Shunju begins in 1986 in Mishuku, Tokyo. I wanted a restaurant where my friends and I could wholeheartedly indulge in food and drink. As Shunju was a completely new, and very personal, concept there was no existing restaurant or *izakaya* (tavern) to take as a role model.

Mishuku was an extremely quiet neighborhood— with hardly any street traffic at that time—so Shunju embarked on its journey with a cargo full of uncertainties. However, rumors of a new hidden retreat spread quickly and young designers from different fields began to gather there. The clientele was young, as Shunju was young. Every day brought new experiences and there was an atmosphere of anticipation of yet another unforeseen experience.

We were both challenged and stimulated by our customers' requests and ideas. Shunju's formative period can best be described as a creative session

between the customers and ourselves. Over fifteen years have passed and Shunju now has five different outlets in Tokyo — Mishuku, Hiroo, Toriizaka, Bunkamura Dori, and Tameike Sanno. Our clientele is much more diversified and we are supported by a large number of faithful customers. Although some say that Shunju has followed the trends over the years, we are not content with such an observation. On the contrary, we believe that new endeavors set the trends and create the times. And we are confident that Shunju is one of them.

architecture Shunju's architecture is undoubtedly one of its strong features. Not only does it excite the younger clientele but it also impresses discerning connoisseurs well versed in Japanese aesthetics. Shunju's architecture is truly unprecedented and is rich in texture and details.

above The majority of the dishware used at Shunju is custom-made or, in some cases, antique. You will notice a wide variety of ceramic styles throughout this book. Handpainted ceramics, such as the dishes above (far left), are called *etsuke*. Stacked *kodaizara* (second from left) display a style derived from ancient ceremonial ware. Bamboo *sake* cups and chopsticks (second from right) are hand-crafted for our forest banquets (*utage*). Dried red chilies sit on Shigaraki dishes (far right), a renowned ceramic region located in Western Japan. Many styles of Japanese ceramics are referred to by the name of the region where they are produced because the variety of clay indigenous to that area determines its texture or color. **opposite** Sake carafes (*tokkuri*) and cups (*guinomi*) are the most highly prized—and often the most expensive—of all hand-thrown Japanese ceramics. Pictured here are those in a white glaze (*kohiki*) and porcelain.

Many people point to the unusual weave of Shunju's architecture. They are referring to the juxtaposition of diversified materials such aged solid wood, bamboo, thick handmade Japanese paper, recycled brick, earthen walls, rusted steel, glass and sparkling stainless. The materials themselves, some traditional, some modern and some unconventional, compose the architectural design. The roughness of the various textures, the mass of volume, and the dull sheen of antiquity constitute Shunju's environment.

These elements are in complete synthesis with one another yet at times are in conflict to create a definite tension. The installation of the various elements, in the bare concrete shell, completes a unity at a distant view but asserts each one's individual existence at a closer view, and is positioned to stimulate the five senses.

bar One distinctive feature of the architecture is the coexistence of a dining area and a bar area. Although this is not a particularly unique feature for Western restaurants, it was a unique feature in a Japanese restaurant in Japan when we first opened. The dining area is named *haru* (spring) taken from the first Chinese character in our name and the bar is named *aki* (autumn) taken from the second character. Chinese characters used in the Japanese language have two pronunciations, one is used for when the characters are used in conjunction, and the other when the characters are used separately. Hence the different pronunciations.

The objective of the bar area is be an authentic bar with a complete stock of malt whiskey, infinite choice of cocktails, cigars, and a wine cellar stocked with wines which we import directly from Italy. As incompatible as it may sound, the antique English or Balinese furniture in our bars are in complete harmony with the antique Korean chests and dining trays as they seem to project the same quality of luster when placed in Shunju's environment.

opposite Agile, experienced hands prepare a sea bream salad in the busy kitchen. right In the *zashiki* (dining room floor) of the Mishuku restaurant is a *ro*, or charcoal pit. Diners sit on the floor with the solid wood ledge surrounding the pit serving as a table. Not only does the *ro* function as an aesthetic highlight, but as a grill for charcoal broiling and, as pictured here, as a heat source for *nabe* (hotpot dinners) on chilly winter evenings.

lighting Like flickering flames, the sharp light projected from the spotlights in the dimly lit interior is reminiscent of the traditional Japanese candles and lanterns. The darkness is a non-existing screen dividing the tables into their own private worlds.

zashiki (dining room floor) The mere act of removing one's shoes and sitting on the floor to dine stimulates the senses for the Japanese. The *zashiki*, the floor dining room, provides the perfect ambience for sharing a hot pot or drinking *sake*.

chashitsu (tearoom) The spirit of my architectural perspective is based on the philosophy of the tea ceremony school. In fact, there is an actual tea room (*chashitsu*), in one of our restaurants, which consolidates this architectural concept into a single unit of space.

Dishware plays a significant role in the presentation of food at Shunju. By sourcing craftsmen skilled in lacquer, bamboo, ceramic and metal work, we have, over the years, designed and developed our own original dishware.

We also practice an aestheticism, *mitatate*, in the tea ceremony—a creative technique of employing completely unexpected things as vessels: glass bottles sliced near the bottom as small glass bowls; the lids of Korean kimchi pots as large platters; metal rakes for leveling ash heated over the grill to serve a sizzling chicken dish.

Recycling traditional ware is also a kind of *mitatate*, such as uncovering the long unused lacquerware sets, traditionally given to the bride by her parents as part of her dowry, and relacquering them in a luscious matte lacquer (*kodaishu*)—the wonderful rebirth of a new ware is thus witnessed.

left The Shunju way of hospitality, *motenashi,* is illustrated when our waiting staff pick the meat out of a crab leg or divide a dish into individual portions for our diners.
opposite The spirit of Sugimoto's architectural perspective is vividly expressed in his interpretation of the *chashitsu,* tearoom, in the Toriizaka restaurant. Diners sit on the *tatami,* flooring woven from rush, and lacquered trays serve as individual dining tables in the tradition of *cha kaiseki,* the meal served in the tea ceremony. The small entrance at the back, *nejiriguchi,* is in the traditional scale designed to lower one's posture when entering the tearoom.

We pray that the tradition of Japanese crafts will continue and thrive and, by continuing to work with these artists and artisans, we believe that we can play a small role in supporting these crafts. We also like to mix various dishware and utensils from other Asian cultures such as Korea, Java, and Vietnam. Some are used as is while others are refinished in Japan. Some are contemporary craftworks, others are period pieces from the Yi Dynasty in Korea or the Edo Period in Japan. All have been carefully selected with the same eye and collectively they express the Shunju style.

hospitality The Shunju way of hospitality—*motenashi* —is to ensure guests' satisfaction is complete by offering them as much information about the food as possible. Taste is not simply a sensory matter for the human palate, but is the memory of an experience that also includes that moment in time and environment.

Conjure up memories of savoring the fish you caught at the river or the wild mushrooms you gathered in the forest and you'll understand what we mean.

Therefore, we feel that is inadequate to simply serve fine ingredients: it is important also to pass on the background of the ingredients for true enjoyment of our dishes. Not only should the chefs be aware of who produces a certain vegetable, where a fish is caught, or how a wild fungus is gathered, but also the consumer. To this end, we provide information about our ingredients and producers in our menus.

Our regular guests are so well-informed they will ask us when the sweetfish (*ayu*) will arrive from Shimanto River, or if the tomato being served is from Yamazaki Farm. The interest focuses on the ingredient, and encompasses much more than the limited confines of the platter. Our menu books account for many interesting conversations at the dining table.

the seasonal kitchen

"The most important element in Shunju's cuisine is to be able to truly appreciate the four seasons and the abundant blessings which mother nature has bestowed upon us. Ultimately, this is what we consider to be the new Japanese cuisine."
— Marcia Iwatate

food for all seasons

Shunju's cuisine begins with the pursuit of the finest ingredients and seasonings available to us. Energetic vegetables free of chemicals grown from seeds harvested from organic crop, free-range chickens which roam the foothills of mountains, soy sauce made from spring water and aged in wooden barrels, sea salt which has been dried by the strong, tropical Okinawan sun, the list is endless.

Our philosophy is to present these ingredients in their purest form. Japan is blessed with four distinctive seasons—we have been bestowed with a lavish variety of food materials and the luxury to savor the best of what each season has to offer, traditionally referred to as *shun* in Japanese. We believe that in order to present this *shun* in its finest form, cooking methods should be kept simple. When we serve *shun* vegetables raw as an appetizer, they are often neither cut nor torn but, rather, served whole with some sea salt and a *miso* dip. Guests are delighted to bite into vegetables which were plucked from the fields that very morning.

The most important element in Shunju's cuisine is to be able to truly appreciate the four seasons and the abundant blessings which mother nature has bestowed upon us. Ultimately, this is what we consider to be the new Japanese cuisine.

The tomato freshly plucked from the fields in the early morning, still glistening with morning dew, is far more delicious than the salad you find in a restaurant. The fisherman's breakfast of freshly caught sashimi on board the boat stirs a greater appetite than the refined fish dish at a well-established *kaiseki* restaurant. There are times when the simple act of procuring one's own food is the ultimate gastronomic experience. The more realistic the experience of knowing what and how one is eating, the better it tastes.

At Shunju, we strive to serve the seasons and regional climates instead of culinary expertise or vanity. The interest focuses on the ingredient, and extends to a realm much greater than that of the limited confines of the platter.

If we are really searching the truth about vegetables, we should first seek knowledge about the soil, for the truth about fish, we should seek knowledge of the fishing ports. So we embark upon our journey leaving behind the pots and pans and travel throughout Japan to discover unknown food materials and regional cuisine that has been passed down for generations.

One of the first things we discover on these journeys is that the talk of the trade is truly superficial. The undiluted voice of the real producers, the farmers and fishermen, is the most relevant source of our education and inspiration.

Shunju's cuisine is supported by a countless number of regional producers. The people that we have encountered on our journeys have become our marketplace. Wonderfully fresh ingredients arrive on a daily basis, and our chefs' only task is to face them in a sincere manner and recognize a dish befitting them.

below Bamboo lanterns (far left) stake out the paths through the trees to the *utage* (forest banquet). A *noren*—a traditional Japanese curtain which marks an entrance—serves as the doorway to the *utage* site (second from left). Onions and *sato imo* (taro potatoes), grill on a charcoal pit (second from right). Campari with freshly squeezed orange juice is served at our al fresco bar (far right). opposite A dining table set for the *utage* (forest banquet) with *sake* cups and chopsticks crafted from freshly cut bamboo, wild flower chopstick pillows and fir branch cushions.

utage As the sun sets, roaring flames from the log fire illuminate the forest. Candles flicker in the freshly cut bamboo stands and scent the air with their fresh aroma. A Balinese xylophone echoes faintly in the background, signaling that the *utage* will commence shortly.

The *utage* is a grand banquet held periodically to entertain valued guests in the most eloquent Shunju style—in montane forest far away from Tokyo. The *utage* commences at dusk, just as the forest begins to darken, echoing the darkness that fills a theater before a performance.

In fact the banquet is very much a theatrical performance in a natural stage setting. Candlesticks, chopsticks, and dishware are fashioned from bamboo, leaves become chopstick rests, hundreds of lanterns made from handmade *washi* paper light the dark mountain paths and lit glass chunks shimmer in the river flowing far below the hanging bridge at the entrance of the site. The whole mountain is transformed into Shunju.

opposite and above A hearty soup is prepared with oxtail and plenty of vegetables to warm our diners in the chilly evening. The *utage* is a major event for us. We repeatedly go to the site to plan the layout and display. No mistakes are allowed in entertaining our most valued guests. The previous day is spent on digging the fire pit, setting up the bar counter, installing the lights, hauling the supplies up the rugged mountain path and cutting the bamboo to make the candle-stands, chopsticks and dishware. The actual day is spent cooking and displaying. Bamboo skewered *iwana* (a river fish), bamboo shoot, *soramame* (broad beans) and white asparagus ready to be grilled on the charcoal pit. The chefs preparing crabs in the makeshift kitchen.

opposite Guests sitting on the *tatami* flooring (woven from rush) set around the charcoal pit, to indulge in the grilled crabs and vegetables. above Hundreds of lanterns made from handmade *washi* paper light the dark mountain paths to the site (far left). The buffet table, improvised from branches cut on site, is laden with crabs (second from left). A solid glass bar counter, complete with *kilim* carpets, is lit by bamboo torches (second from right). Preparing the *utage* is truly a race against time and year after year we find ourselves rushing about madly to get everything finished (far right).

Our clients from Tokyo have reached the hanging bridge, the logs and candles are immediately lit and the banquet commences with a big roar of fire and our greetings of welcome.

When the guests cross the bridge they are met by the sight and aroma of crabs and vegetables grilling on an immense fire pit, soup bubbling in a large cauldron, and large platters laden with home-smoked duck, pickled beets, whole raw vegetables with sea salt and *miso* dips, and homemade pickles.

We catch glimpses of our guests laughing, drinking and devouring the various dishes by the flickering flames of the candles and fire pit. This is the essence of our *utage*. The genuine experience of eating— of indulging oneself to one's heart's content—in a natural environment such as this, is to experience life itself.

When the roaring flames have turned to red coals and the ambience mellows, it is time for the banquet to come to a close. It gives us great pleasure to hear our parting guests say that they would like the evening to continue forever. We share those same lingering thoughts and sorrow of parting.

The *utage* is a major event for us. It really is hard work but we thoroughly enjoy ourselves and, ultimately, that is what it's all about. Enjoy!

spring

Spring is the season of new life, the beginning of a New Year in the lunar calendar. Wild vegetables peek out from the mountain soil, spring cabbages shine in the morning sun, and new green tea leaves perfume the air with their splendid fra... *Wasabi*, which only grows in the pure mountain spring waters, is one such seasonal bless... no Spring vegetable is more eagerly awaited ... the bamboo shoot.

As the days slowly grow warmer, bamboo shoots are the only things on our minds, for the shoots must be harvested just as they peek out from the ground. Our eager thoughts drive us to the telephone as early as in February. We are calling the parents of one of our colleagues who own a mountain covered in lush bamboo forests in Shizuoka Prefecture. Weather conditions significantly affect the growth of the shoots. They tend to shoot up earlier when there has been abundant rainfall. We generally receive the long awaited call in early March. There is no doubt that spring arrives to Shunju along with this joyful tiding and we speed off to Shizuoka after midnight, having closed the restaurants.

Preserving the freshness of bamboo shoot is a highly delicate operation. You can actually see a shoot start to oxidize, discolor, and turn bitter from the moment that it is dug out. It is truly a race against time to preserve the refreshing "newborn" taste. Normally, harvested shoots are whisked off to the gourmet markets in refrigerated trucks as a highly coveted delicacy, known as *asabori* ("morning dug"). This system is seemingly the best means for competing against time but it can not prevent the oxidation and marked decline in taste. Once they reach the kitchen, the shoots must still be boiled with rice bran and dried chili peppers to remove the bitterness.

We immediately begin to boil the shoots on site in an iron cauldron full of spring water to halt the oxidation process and to trap the flavor before it deteriorates. We have no need for the additional ingredients as no bitterness has set in. Digging in the forest and clamoring around the cauldron is a customary Shunju spring ritual for us. Of course, we rush back to Tokyo in order to serve this treasured harvest that very evening.

above left to right The harvested shoots are immediately taken down for boiling by a tiny monorail. *Negi bozu* (blossoms of the Japanese bunching onion) in the morning sun. The boiled shoots being raised from the cauldron. Staff driving down the steep digging site with the harvest. The bamboo tofu ware is made on site. Staff hard at work: it takes an expert foot to feel the shoots hidden under a carpet of bamboo leaves.

Grilled bamboo shoots
Takenoko no ippon yaki
筍の一本焼き

Serves 4
2 12-in (30-cm) *takenoko* (fresh bamboo shoots) (for preparation see page 253)
1/4 cup (60 ml) *koikuchi shoyu* (soy sauce)

If you have the opportunity to dig bamboo shoots fresh from the ground, we recommend charcoal grilling them on the spot in their outer skins. Freshly dug shoots have a high water content so they steam in their skins when grilled. You will never forget their sweet, delicate flavor and indescribable texture, which is totally different to that of canned or vacuum-packed shoots. This extravagant way of savoring the spring delicacy is a treat which we reward ourselves with after a strenuous morning of digging.

1 Prepare the charcoal; the coals are ready when all glow orange-red.
2 Carefully place the bamboo shoots directly into the red hot charcoal and cover completely with coals. Grill for about 15 minutes, do not worry about the skin becoming charred. Remove from the charcoal and test for doneness. Pierce the thick bottom of a bamboo shoot with a metal skewer and keep it there for 5 seconds before removing. If the skewer is hot, but not too hot to touch (about 120°F or 40°C), return the bamboo shoot on top of the charcoal, brush evenly with soy sauce, and grill for another 5 minutes. If the metal skewer is not hot enough, return to the charcoal, cook for a further 5 minutes, and repeat the process before brushing with the soy sauce.
3 Place each bamboo shoot on a cutting board, then slice in half lengthwise. Remove the shoot from the skin and slice crosswise into bite-sized pieces. Discard the most charred outer skins, then arrange the remaining skin into its original form and arrange the bamboo shoot on the skin. Serve immediately.

Bamboo shoot rice cooked in a stone pot

Takenoko meshi no ishi gama daki

筍飯の石釜炊き

Serves 4

2 teaspoons vegetable oil
1/4 *taka no tsume* (dried hot red chili)
2 oz (60 g) *takenoko* (fresh bamboo shoots (for preparation see page 253), sliced into batons 2 in (5 cm) long and 1/2 in (5 mm) thick; substitute with vacuum-packed boiled whole bamboo shoot
1 teaspoon natural sea salt
1/3 cup (90 ml) *katsuo dashi* (bonito stock) (for preparation see page 248)
1 teaspoon white sesame seeds
1 cup (200 g) Japanese rice (see page 260 for washing instructions)
3/4 cup (200 ml) water
2 tablespoons Korean virgin sesame oil

The most popular way of serving bamboo shoot is to cook it with rice or braise it with seaweed. As you will notice throughout this book, we have borrowed many ideas and ingredients from Korean cuisine, and the stone pot is one of the most important of these, along with aromatic Korean virgin sesame oil. Although we cook many of our flavored rice dishes, as well as plain rice, in a stone pot—it cooks excellent rice and produces a nice crunchy crust— any heavy-bottomed enameled pot will do the trick.

1 Heat the vegetable oil in a saucepan over low heat and sauté the red chili. Add the bamboo shoot batons and increase heat to high. Add the salt and continue to sauté until the bamboo shoot baton is slightly browned. Stir continuously with a wooden spatula to prevent the shoots burning on the bottom of the pan.
2 When the bamboo shoot batons are slightly browned, add bonito stock and bring to a boil. Lower the heat and simmer until most of the liquid is reduced. Add the sesame seeds, check for seasoning, and set aside to cool.
3 Place the washed rice and water in a stone pot, cover, and bring to a boil over high heat. When it reaches a rolling boil, remove from the heat and leave to stand for 10 minutes. Then return to high heat for

5 minutes. This develops a delicious crunchy crust at the bottom of the pot. If you do not own a stone pot, cook the rice following the instructions on page 260. Allow to stand for 10 minutes, then heat over high heat for a further 5 minutes.
4 Open the lid and slowly drizzle sesame oil around the inside wall of the pot. Leave to stand for a few minutes, then add the sautéed bamboo shoot. Carry the stone pot to the table—be sure to wear thick oven gloves and use a stand or mat to protect the table as the pot becomes extremely hot.
5 Stir the rice at the table and divide into individual rice bowls. Make sure that every bowl gets some of the deliciously pungent crunchy crust and some bamboo shoot batons.

Deep-fried bamboo shoots with dried bonito flakes

Takenoko no tosa age

筍の土佐揚げ

Serves 4
1 egg
6-in (15-cm) *takenoko* (fresh bamboo shoots) (for preparation see page 253); substitute with vacuum-packed boiled whole bamboo shoot
2 tablespoons *bai niku* (salted plum paste)
1 1/2 cups (15 g) *kezuri bushi* (dried bonito flakes)
6 cups (1 1/2 liters) vegetable oil
8 *kinome* (young *sansho* leaves), to garnish

Zukushi is to indulge in one ingredient, to prepare a full-course meal consisting entirely of that one food item. If you are fortunate enough to have access to fresh bamboo shoots, try preparing a full-course meal using bamboo shoots and prepare this dish for one of the courses.

1 Beat the egg in a bowl large enough for dipping the bamboo shoot slices.
2 Slice the bamboo shoot lengthwise into 4 wedges. Make a lengthwise incision on the thick part of the wedge, about 1/2 in (1 cm) deep. Using a knife, spread the salted plum paste into this incision.
3 Put the bonito shavings in a saucepan over low heat and crumple them with your hands so they dry further and break into fine pieces. Place in a flat container large enough to roll the bamboo shoot slices.

4 Pour the vegetable oil in a saucepan and heat to 325°F (160°C). Dip the bamboo shoot wedges into the egg and coat evenly. Next, coat each wedge evenly with the bonito shavings, then carefully slip into the oil and deep-fry. Turn the bamboo shoots occasionally so that they are fried evenly. When nicely browned, remove from the oil with a slotted spoon. Gently shake above the pan to remove any excess oil and drain on paper towels. Serve immediately, garnished with fresh *kinome* leaves.

Bamboo shoot sashimi

Takenoko no sashimi

筍の刺身

Serves 4

4 teaspoons *sake*

8 teaspoons *koikuchi shoyu* (soy sauce)

6-in (15-cm) *takenoko* (fresh bamboo shoots) (for preparation see page 253)

2 sprigs *kinome* (young *sansho* leaves), to garnish

1 teaspoon fresh wasabi, grated, substitute with frozen fresh or tube wasabi

Koikuchi shoyu (soy sauce), to accompany wasabi

The name of this recipe says sashimi but, in fact, the bamboo shoot is not served raw. It is referred to as sashimi because this dish can only be made if you have freshly dug bamboo shoots, hence in the same context as having immaculately fresh seafood. The sweet flavor and crunchy texture is indescribable.

1 Pour *sake* into a saucepan and bring to a boil over high heat to boil off the alcohol content. Cool and combine with soy sauce. Set aside.

2 Slice the bamboo shoot lengthwise into thin slices, about 3/4 in (2 cm) thick. Arrange on a serving platter and garnish with fresh *kinome* sprigs. Place the grated wasabi on the platter and serve with soy sauce in a separate dish.

Bamboo shoots braised with seaweed

Takenoko no wakame ni

筍の若布煮

Serves 4

12-in (30-cm) *takenoko* (fresh bamboo shoots, for preparation see page 253), substitute with vacuum-packed boiled whole bamboo shoot

3 cups (750 ml) *katsuo dashi* (bonito stock) (for preparation see page 248)

1/3 cup (90 ml) *sake*

1/3 cup (90 ml) *mirin*

1/3 cup (90 ml) *usukuchi shoyu* (light soy sauce)

2 teaspoons natural sea salt

10 oz (300 g) fresh *wakame* seaweed, substitute with dried *wakame* (reconstituted in cold water for several minutes) or salt preserved *wakame* (soaked in cold water for 1 hour)

This recipe is the most traditional and the most popular way to enjoy the spring delicacy, bamboo shoot. Although there is no real substitute for the delicate aroma and crunchy texture of fresh bamboo shoots, you may use vacuum-packed boiled whole bamboo shoots, sold in Japanese grocery stores, if the fresh variety is hard to come by.

1 Slice the top half of the bamboo shoot lengthwise into 6 wedges. Slice the tougher bottom half across in 3/4-in (2-cm) slices or, if the shoot is very thick, slice the round slices across in half to form semicircles.
2 Place the round (or semicircular) slices, bonito stock, and seasonings in a saucepan. Bring to a boil over high heat, then reduce the heat to low, and simmer until the bamboo shoot is slightly colored. Add the bamboo shoot wedges and simmer for another 1 hour.
3 Blanch the *wakame* briefly, drain, and place in the center of a serving bowl. Arrange the bamboo shoots on top and pour on some of the cooking liquid. Serve immediately.

Spring mountain vegetable tempura

Sansai no tempura

山菜の天ぷら

Serves 4

8 *taranome* (angelica tree shoots), about 3 oz (80 g)

8 *urui* (hosta shoots), about 1 oz (30 g)

8 *nobiru* (red garlic), about 1 oz (30 g)

8 *fukinoto* (unopened buds of Japanese butterbur), about 2 oz (65 g)

8 young green tea leaves

8 *kogomi* (fiddleheads), about 1 1/2 oz (50 g)

8 *koshiabura* (unopened buds of the L. *acanthopanax sciadophylloides* tree), about 1 oz (30 g)

4 cups (1 liter) vegetable oil

1 cup (100 g) all-purpose (plain) flour, for dusting

Natural sea salt to taste

Batter

1 egg yolk

2 cups (500 ml) iced water

2 cups (240 g) all-purpose (plain) flour, sifted and chilled

Like bamboo shoots, *sansai* or mountain vegetables are a spring favorite, although some *sansai* are eaten in the fall. Many varieties of *sansai* are now cultivated but their flavor cannot compare to that of the wild varieties plucked from the mountain side, which have a distinct bitter taste (time is of essence though as these fresh vegetables become increasingly bitter as they oxidize). Although it is difficult to find *sansai* outside of Japan and Korea, you may substitute other bitter greens and vegetables such as dandelion, mustard, endives, scallion, and so forth. As tempura is time-consuming to fry, and tastes best when freshly deep-fried, many Japanese families make tempura at the dining table over a halogen tabletop range, or a portable gas stove.

1 Remove any browned or discolored sections from the vegetables.

2 To prepare the batter, beat the egg yolk thoroughly with the iced water. Add the chilled flour. Stir briefly with thick chopsticks, but do not mix to a smooth batter, as tempura batter should always contain lumps of flour. Place the bowl with the batter over a larger bowl filled with iced water to keep the batter cold.

3 Pour the vegetable oil into a saucepan until it reaches 6 in (15 cm) in depth and heat to 325°F (160°C). Spread flour for dusting in a baking pan or a flat, shallow container. Lightly dust each vegetable with a coating of flour.

4 Carefully dip in the batter and deep-fry. Turn the vegetables occasionally so that they are evenly fried. Once lightly browned and they float quickly to the surface when pushed down with chopsticks, remove from the oil with a slotted spoon. Gently shake above the pan to remove any excess oil and drain on paper towels. Serve immediately with some natural sea salt.

Spring starters
Haru no otoshi
春のお通し

As with all the starters for each season, the individual dishes can be substituted or improvised using leftover dishes or food materials. These starters are titbits that should be beautifully presented to start the conversation before dinner. The presentation is borrowed from the Buddhist monk's dining table in Korea. For the remaining spring starter recipes, see page 71.

Braised sea bream roe (Tai ko no fukume ni)
1-in (2 1/2-cm) ginger, peeled
1/2 cup (120 ml) katsuo dashi (bonito stock) (for preparation see page 248)
2 teaspoons usukuchi shoyu (light soy sauce)
2 teaspoons mirin
Pinch natural sea salt
3 oz (80 g) tai ko (sea bream roe)

(prepare 1 day in advance)
1 Thinly slice the ginger, then cut these slices into needle thin slivers.
2 Combine the ginger, stock, light soy sauce, mirin, and salt in a low dish.
3 Cut the sea bream roe across into 4 or 5 pieces and blanch in boiling water; they will "bloom" and become fluffy. Remove carefully with a slotted spoon and place in the combined broth. Leave to marinate for 1 day before serving.

Welsh onion salad (Jako negi salada)
4 teaspoons ponzu sauce (see page 57)
4 teaspoons Korean virgin sesame oil
4 teaspoons koikuchi shoyu (soy sauce)
1/3 oz (10 g) jako (baby air-cured anchovies)
20 stalks fugu negi (welsh or ciboule onion), substitute with green stalks of thin scallions (spring onions)

1 Cut the welsh onions or scallions into 1 1/4-in (3-cm) lengths.
2 Combine the ponzu sauce, sesame oil, and soy sauce to make the dressing.
3 Toss the welsh onions or scallions with the dressing, arrange in a small bowl, and garnish with baby anchovies.

Blanched Japanese butterbur (Fuki no fukume ni)
2 fuki (stalks Japanese butterbur), substitute with celery
3 pinches natural sea salt
2 teaspoons koikuchi shoyu (soy sauce)
2 tablespoons katsuo dashi (bonito stock) (for preparation see page 248)
2 teaspoons mirin

(prepare 1 day in advance)
1 Rub the butterbur with salt until it becomes more pliable.
2 Bring some water to a boil in a saucepan, then add the butterbur and boil, over medium heat, for 2 minutes. Drain and refresh in iced water. Peel off the thin outer skin.
3 Combine the butterbur, sea salt, soy sauce, bonito stock, and mirin in a saucepan and bring to a boil over medium heat. When it reaches a boil, remove from heat and leave aside to cool. Cut the butterbur into 2-in (5-cm) pieces, then return to the broth and soak for 1 day before serving.

Blanched water dropwort (Seri no ni oroshi)
1/2 cup (120 ml) katsuo dashi (bonito stock) (for preparation see page 248)
2 teaspoons usukuchi shoyu (light soy sauce)
2 teaspoons mirin
Pinch natural sea salt
Few drops Korean virgin sesame oil
5 oz (150 g) seri (water dropwort), substitute with watercress, washed

(prepare 2–3 hours in advance)
1 Bring some salted water to a boil in a saucepan and briefly blanch the dropwort; then refresh in iced water. Cut across into 1-in (2 1/2-cm) lengths.
2 Combine the stock, light soy sauce, mirin, salt, and sesame oil in a small bowl and add the water dropwort. Marinate 2–3 hours before serving.

Rape Shoots Dressed with Mustard (Nano Hana No Karashi Ae)
10 stalks rape shoots (nano hana) substitute with broccoli
1/3 oz (10 g) powdered Japanese mustard (wagarashi ko)
2 teaspoons soy sauce (koikuchi)
2 tablespoons bonito stock
2 teaspoons mirin

1 Wash the rape shoots thoroughly.
2 Boil some water with salt in a saucepan, blanch the rape shoots until tender and refresh in ice water. Cut crosswise into about 4 sections.
3 Combine all the ingredients to make the dressing.
4 Toss the rape shoots with the dressing. Adjust the amount of mustard depending upon how spicy you like it.

Green and lavender tofu squares
Masu dofu
升豆腐

Serves 4

Green tofu
2/3 cup (150 ml) green soymilk (see page 255)
1 teaspoon *nigari* (bittern), see Note

Lavender tofu
2/3 cup (150 ml) black soymilk (see page 255)
1 teaspoon *nigari* (bittern), see Note

Condiments
2 2/3 oz (80 g) *naga negi* (long welsh onion), cut in thin slivers and refreshed in cold water (see page 251), substitute with white part of scallion (spring onion)
1 1/3 oz (40 g) *shiso* (perilla) leaves, cut in thin slivers and refreshed in cold water (see page 251)
Koikuchi shoyu (soy sauce)

4 *masu* or square wooden boxes (83 x 83 x 57 mm)

Tofu is undoubtedly one of the most representative dishes of Shunju. Our tofu is made daily—soymilk is curdled with *nigari* (bittern)—in different ware unique to each of our five restaurants; in this case in *masu* (traditional square, wooden measuring cups). We had discovered a delicious handmade tofu in Kyoto, but despite the availability of (costly) refrigerated transportation, there was simply no comparison to the taste of freshly made and delivered tofu. The only answer to our dilemma was the usual Shunju spirit of "whatver is unavailable, we make or find ourselves," hence our latest tofu recipe using soy milk extracted from green and black soybeans.

1 Prepare the basic soymilk by following steps 1 through 8 on page 254, substituting green and then black soybeans for the regular soybeans. The soymilk recipe on page 254 yields more than is needed for this dish, so either make more for a large dinner, or make only one color at a time.
2 Pour the soymilk into a saucepan and heat over medium heat. Stir continuously with a wooden or bamboo spatula, scraping the bottom of the pan as you do it, to prevent the milk from burning.
3 When the soymilk reaches 140°F (60°C), pour it into the bamboo container, add *nigari* and stir quickly. Remove the spoon once the soymilk starts to coagulate. Chill in the refrigerator.
4 Place the refreshed welsh onion and *shiso* leaf slivers in a small dish and serve with the soy sauce as a condiment.

Note: *Nigari* (bittern) is the coagulent used to make tofu. Traditionally, it is made from the residue (magnesium chloride) of the salt-making process but, today, chemical coagulents are usually used. Natural (and artificial) *nigari* is available from Japanese grocery stores or you can make your own by boiling down 3 quarts (3 liters) of seawater over high heat for about 2 hours until salt crystals start to appear. When the crystals start to gather into larger crystals, the liquid on the top is the *nigari*. This method will yield about 4 1/2 tablespoons *nigari*. Cool in the pot, then scoop the surface of the settled *nigari*, and pour through a fine sieve lined with paper towel or cheese cloth. If you do not live by the ocean, dissolve 1 1/2 teaspoons Epsom salts in 1 cup (250 ml) water and use about one-third of this solution.

Green bean soymilk yuba

Ryokuto nama yuba

緑豆生湯葉

Serves 4
Pinch natural sea salt
13 1/2 oz (420 g) *endomame* (shelled green peas), substitute with *edamame* (podded green soybeans) or *soramame* (fava/broad beans)
5 cups (1 1/4 liters) homemade soymilk (see page 254)
2 tablespoons fresh wasabi, substitute with frozen fresh or tube wasabi
Koikuchi shoyu (soy sauce)

Yuba, a famous Kyoto delicacy, is the film that forms on the surface when soymilk is heated, somewhat akin to the film which forms on the surface of heated milk. This film absorbs the majority of the protein contained in soymilk and, at over 52 percent, is the richest source of protein known to exist. Nearly all fresh *yuba* is produced in Kyoto but due to its labor intensive method of production and the high refrigerated transportation costs, it tends to be very expensive. At Shunju, we are able to make our own *yuba* because of the abundant amount of soymilk that we extract for our home-made tofu. In this recipe, we have made our own green version with a green bean purée. It will keep refrigerated for one day.

1 Bring a pan of salted water to a boil and cook the shelled green peas until tender. Drain.
2 Transfer the peas to a blender and add one-quarter of the soymilk. Blend until the peas are finely ground. Pour the mixture through a fine sieve and mash any remaining bits. Pour scant 1/2 cup (100 ml) of this green soymilk into a flat non-reactive container (such as tupperware) and set aside.
3 Pour the rest of the green soymilk mixture and the remaining plain soymilk into a pot and heat over medium heat, scraping the bottom of the pot, to prevent it from burn-ing. When it reaches 176°F (80°C), remove from the heat and wait for the *yuba* to form on the surface. You can leave it and check on it from time to time. (See page 254.)
4 Lift the film out carefully with chopsticks and soak in the reserved green soymilk. Make sure that the surface of the film is completely coated to prevent it from drying out. Heat the soymilk again and repeat this procedure until no more *yuba* forms. Discard remaining soymilk.
5 Cover the *yuba* soaking in the green soymilk with plastic wrap or a lid, and chill in the refrigerator. Serve chilled with freshly grated wasabi and soy sauce (see page 255).

Sea bream salad

Tai no kaisen salada

鯛の海鮮サラダ

Serves 1

1/2 *kyuri* (Japanese cucumber), about 1 1/2 oz (20 g); substitute with English cucumber
1/2 small carrot, about 2/3 oz (20 g)
3/4-oz (20-g) *naga negi* (long welsh onion), substitute with white part of scallion (spring onion)
2 1/4 oz (70 g) radish
6 1/2 oz (200 g) sea bream
1 egg, lightly beaten
Oil for preparing omelet

Salad dressing
1/2 clove garlic
Pinch minced ginger
3/4 oz (20 g) *naga negi* (long welsh onion), substitute with white part of scallion (spring onion)
1 heaped tablespoon *kochujang* (Korean red chili paste), or to taste
3 tablespoons vegetable oil
Pinch natural sea salt
3 tablespoons *ponzu* sauce (available bottled, or see recipe below)

Ponzu sauce
5 tablespoons *sake*
1 1/2 cups (360 ml) *koikuchi shoyu* (soy sauce)
1 1/2 cups (360 ml) fresh or bottled *kabosu* juice (a kind of citrus, L. *citrus sphaerocarpa*), substitute with fresh lemon juice
1 handful *kezuri bushi* (dried bonito flakes)
2 *sudachi* (small acidic citrus fruit), halved, substitute with lemons
4 x 7-in (10 x 18-cm) sheet *konbu* (kelp), gently wiped clean (leaving the flavorful white powder on the *konbu*)

Tangy and light, this refreshing dish is perfect for spring. If you live in Japan, be sure to ask for *tennen dai* (wild sea bream). Although it is more expensive than the normal farmed sea bream (*tai*), you will taste the difference. You can substitute sea bream with other firm-fleshed white fish, just make sure the fish is absolutely fresh. You can determine the freshness of fish by the firmness of its flesh, the sheen of its scales and eyes, the firm adherence of the scales, and by the bright red color of its gills or the translucent, shimmering color of its flesh.

1 To prepare the salad dressing, mince together the garlic, ginger, and *naga negi*, transfer the mixture to a bowl, and stir in the remaining dressing ingredients. Set aside.
2 Slice the cucumber, carrot, and *naga negi* into needle-thin slivers and refresh in cold water (see page 251). Cut the radish into paper-thin slices and refresh this too in cold water.
3 Prepare the sea bream into a three-section fillet (see page 244) and *sogi giri* cut (see page 247). Place the sea bream on your cutting board skin side up, the thinner side closer to you. Slice into 3/4-in (1 1/2-cm) thick slices by slicing on a diagonal slant. Arrange slices in a circular pattern on the dish.
4 Pour the egg into a lightly oiled skillet and make a very thin omelet. Remove from the skillet, cool, then roll and slice into needle-thin slivers.
5 Lightly toss the vegetable slivers together and pile high on top of the

sea bream slices and garnish with the egg slivers.
6 Pour the dressing on the salad just before serving.

Ponzu sauce
1 In a saucepan, bring *sake* to a boil over high heat to burn off the alcohol. Remove from heat and cool.
2 In a sealable container, or a widemouthed bottle, large enough to accommodate all the liquid, pour the soy sauce and *kabosu* juice and mix thoroughly. Add the cooled *sake*, bonito flakes, and *konbu*. Squeeze the liquid from the *sudachi* into the container, then add in the squeezed fruit.
3 Let the sauce rest in a cool place or in the refrigerator overnight. Strain through a fine sieve or cheesecloth. This recipe yields about 3 cups (800 ml) *ponzu* sauce and will keep for 2 months refrigerated.

Clam and udo salad
Aoyagi to udo no aemono
青柳とうどの和え物

Serves 4
1 stalk *udo*, about 1 lb (500 g),
  substitute with white asparagus
2 teaspoons *su* (rice vinegar)
8 sashimi-quality *akagai* (fresh hen
  clams), about 3 oz (80 g), shelled,
  rinsed, and sliced lengthwise into
  3 pieces
8 *shiso* (perilla) leaves
1 oz (25 g) *menegi* (welsh onion
  sprouts), substitute with chives

Salad dressing
4 teaspoons *koikuchi shoyu* (soy sauce)
1 tablespoon fresh wasabi, substitute
  with frozen fresh or tube wasabi
8 teaspoons vegetable oil

Like all other shellfish except abalone, *aoyagi*—or hen clam—is a spring delicacy. It is blanched briefly, then tossed in a simple dressing with another spring delicacy, *udo*, a stalk plant somewhat similar in taste and fragrance to white asparagus. Wild *udo* belongs to the category of *sansai*, or spring mountain vegetables, but the *udo* used in this recipe is the cultivated variety, possessing a milder flavor which does not overpower the shellfish. Because it is grown in the dark, it has a snow-white color.

1 Cut the *udo* into 1 1/2-in (4-cm) lengths and peel. Slice each piece in half lengthwise, then each half lengthwise into thin slices, and finally the thin slices into matchstick slivers. Soak in some water with vinegar added to remove the acid.
2 To make the dressing, combine the soy sauce, wasabi, and vegetable oil. Set aside.

3 Blanch the clams in hot water, about 190°F (80°C), and refresh in iced water.
4 Toss the clams and *udo* with the dressing, divide into 8 portions, and arrange each portion on a *shiso* leaf. Garnish with *menegi* or chives.

Sea eel braised with spring burdock root

Anago to shin gobo ni

穴子と新牛蒡煮

Serves 4

11 oz (320 g) sashimi-quality *anago* (fillet of conger eel), substitute with other eel or any firm-fleshed white fish (but not with braised eel commonly found in Japanese grocery stores)

6 1/2 oz (200 g) burdock root, soaked in water with a little vinegar

1 1/4 cups (300 ml) *katsuo dashi* (bonito stock) (for preparation see page 248)

2 tablespoons *koikuchi shoyu* (soy sauce)

3 1/2 tablespoons *mirin*

Ginger juice, obtained by peeling, grating, and squeezing ginger

This is a wonderfully light braised spring dish. The burdock root is rich in dietary fiber and vitamins but it is bitter and should always be soaked in water with vinegar before using. The shavings should just be lightly braised so that they retain their crunchy texture. *Anago*, conger eel, is quite rich in fat and compliments the burdock root well.

1 Place the eel on a cutting board above the sink, skin side up, and pour boiling water evenly over it. Remove any slime from the skin by running the spine (the blunt side) of a knife over the skin.

2 Wash and peel the burdock root by scrubbing it, then shave it (as you would sharpen a pencil) with a knife, turning it slowly until you have shaved the entire root. Soak the shavings in water for 10 minutes, then drain and reserve.

3 In a saucepan large enough to fit the eel, bring the stock, soy sauce, and *mirin* to a boil over medium heat. Reduce the heat to low, add the eel (if the eel is too long, cut it in half), and simmer for 5 minutes.

4 Remove the eel carefully so that it does not break. Cut across into bite-size pieces. Arrange in serving bowl, pile the braised burdock root on top, add the ginger juice to the remaining liquid, and slowly pour on top. Serve immediately.

Grilled fava beans and new onions

Yaki soramame to shin tamanegi

焼き天豆と新玉葱

Serves 4
8 *soramame* (fava/broad beans) in their
    pods
Natural sea salt
3 new onions, about 10 oz (300 g) each

In Japan, fava (broad) beans, or *soramame* (literally "heavenly beans"), are an important spring vegetable. They are normally boiled in salt water out of their pods, but at Shunju, where charcoal grilling is an important method of cooking, we have discovered that these beans are delicious grilled in their pods. The heat is trapped and, consequently, the beans are steamed to perfection inside their pods. The same holds true for the sweet new onions which also arrive in spring.

1 Soak the fava beans in their pods in water for a few minutes, then sprinkle them liberally with salt.
2 Remove any wilted outer skins from the onion but be sure to leave the rest of the skin intact.
3 Grill the beans and onions on a charcoal grill or broil under an oven grill until their skin is charred and they are soft to touch, or are easily pierced with a skewer. You should grill the onions first as they take longer to cook.
4 Alternatively, bake the beans and onions in a 350°F (180°C, gas 4) oven, 10 minutes for the onions, and about 5 minutes for the beans.
5 Serve piping hot with some sea salt on the side, or with the spicy miso dip (see page 94).

Ark shell sashimi with grated Japanese yam and vinegar

Aka gai no tororo jitate

赤貝のとろろ仕立て

Serves 4

1/4 cup (60 ml) *su* (rice vinegar)
2 tablespoons *koikuchi shoyu* (soy sauce)
2 tablespoons *mirin*
12 sashimi-quality *aka gai* (ark shells)
Natural sea salt
8 *nano hana* (rape shoots), substitute with broccoli, blanched in salted water and refreshed
6 1/2 oz (200 g) *yamato imo* (Japanese yam), peeled and grated (optional)
Sliver-cut *kizami nori* (laver), substitute with normal *nori* (laver) torn with your fingers (optional)
7 teaspoons (10 g) fresh wasabi, substitute with frozen fresh or tube wasabi

Ark shells, also known as blood clams due to their red flesh, can grow up to 5 in (12 cm) in diameter. As with all other shellfish—with the exception of abalone—they are considered a spring delicacy. You might have seen your sushi chef slap one onto his cutting board and watch it curl up. This procedure is to determine its freshness. Omit the Japanese yam if it is not available or if you are not fond of its slippery texture.

1 Bring the rice vinegar, soy sauce, and *mirin* to a boil in a saucepan over medium heat. Remove from the heat and cool. Chill in refrigerator when completely cooled.
2 Place ark shells in a bowl and gently rub them with some natural sea salt. Rinse them under running water, pat dry with paper towel, and slice in half. Take the thinner half, make an incision in its thicker portion, and slap it onto a cutting board. This makes it open up into a shape resembling a hand.
3 Make a crosshatch pattern on the remaining half by scoring it with diagonal lines using a very sharp knife, then turning it and scoring diagonally across the lines already made.
4 Spoon the grated yam into the bottom of a serving bowl, arrange ark shells and rape shoots on top, then pour the chilled sauce on top. Garnish with the laver slivers and grated wasabi if desired.

Halfbeak sashimi layered with salted plum sauce

Sayori no bai niku kasane zukuri

さよりの梅肉重ね造り

Serves 4

1/2 *shiro uri* (Oriental pickling melon), substitute with Western cucumber

2 sashimi-quality *sayori* (halfbeak fish), substitute with any firm-fleshed white fish

2 sheets white *konbu* (white dried kelp), substitute with *oboro konbu* (shaved, presoaked kelp), or omit

1 heaped tablespoon *bai niku* (salted plum paste)

Salt

Koikuchi shoyu (soy sauce)

Fresh wasabi, substitute with frozen fresh or tube wasabi

Sayori, or halfbeak, is a very long and lean white fish—similar in appearance to gar—which is in season in spring. Here, the fish is layered with salted plum paste. You may substitute halfbeak with other firm-fleshed white fish but make sure the fish is absolutley fresh. The bone garnish may be omitted if you dislike the way it looks but it's full of calcium, delicious, and has a crunchy texture.

1 Cut the pickling melon in half lengthwise and discard the seeds. Lightly sprinkle with salt and set aside.

2 Fillet one fish into three sections (see page 244), ensuring that the backbone is removed with the head and tail attached. Fillet the second fish into five sections (see page 246), removing the backbone but this time discarding the head and tail. Sprinkle the removed backbones with salt and air-dry for 3 hours.

3 Wrap and tie the first backbone (with the attached head and tail) around a flame-proof circular object, such as a round cookie cutter. The other backbone should be left flat. Grill both backbones over low heat on a charcoal grill or gently broil them under an oven grill.

5 Using tweezers, remove any fine bones from the two-section fillet, taking care not to break the flesh. Place the fillet, skin side up, on a cutting board and remove the skin from the head side by pulling it off with your fingers. Spread plum paste on the inner side of the fillet and sandwich the white *konbu*. Transfer to a flat container, cover with plastic wrap, and refrigerate for 15 minutes.

6 Remove the skin from the four-section fillet in the same way. Refrigerate.

7 Cut the sandwiched fillets across into 3 equal slices, stack them into a single pile, and slice across into strips about 5 mm thick.

8 Place the gourd on a serving platter and arrange two-thirds of the sandwiched fish strips in the gourd with the cross-section facing forward.

9 Place a piece of white *konbu* on the serving dish, with the circular backbone on top. Arrange the remaining sandwiched strips on the plate and place the remaining backbone on top. Arrange the five-section fillets next to the circular bone. These fillets can be eaten with soy sauce and wasabi.

Sesame-coated green asparagus

Grin asupara no goma yaki

グリーンアスパラの胡麻焼き

Serves 4

12 green asparagus (medium width), washed thoroughly, lower stalk snapped off, outer skin peeled if necessary

12 paper-thin pork slices (about 7 in by 3 in), long enough to spiral wrap the asparagus, substitute with bacon or *prosciutto* (if too thin, you may use two slices of pork to wrap the asparagus)

Natural sea salt

Freshly ground white pepper

1 cup (100 g) all-purpose (plain) flour

5 oz (150 g) white sesame seeds

2 eggs, beaten thoroughly

2 tablespoons vegetable oil

14 teaspoons (20 g) *wagarashi ko* (powdered Japanese mustard) mixed with 2 1/2 tablespoons hot water to form a smooth paste

1/4 cup (60 ml) *koikuchi shoyu* (soy sauce)

Asparagus is not a traditional Japanese vegetable but is now being cultivated in Hokkaido in the northern part of Japan. This recipe brings a variety of flavors and textures to the sometimes bland asparagus. The crunchy sesame coating is mouth-watering and can, of course, be prepared without pork if you wish.

1 Preheat oven to 350°F (180°C, gas 4).

2 Wrap the asparagus tightly with the pork by starting at the lower end and spiraling up to the tips. Squeeze in your hands so that the pork adheres well. Season the wrapped asparagus with salt and pepper.

3 Spread the flour and sesame separately in flat, shallow containers. Beat the eggs thoroughly and pour into a third flat container that can fit the length of the asparagus. Roll the asparagus in the flour, pat off any excess, dip it in the egg, and finally roll it in the sesame seeds to coat evenly. When the sesame coating has firmed, transfer to an oiled baking sheet.

4 Bake in the oven for 4–5 minutes. If the stalks are very long, slice in half crosswise. Serve immediately, with the mustard and soy sauce in small dishes on the side.

Crab crisps
Kani senbei
かにせんべい

Serves 4
1/2 cup (100 g) cream cheese, at room
   temperature
1/2 cup (70 g) king or snow crabmeat
2 tablespoons mayonnaise
1/4 cup (20 g) dried breadcrumbs
1 teaspoon *koikuchi shoyu* (soy sauce)
Pinch natural sea salt
Pinch cayenne pepper
Pinch white pepper
4 spring roll wrappers

This is one of our popular nibble foods, which we serve in the bar as well as in the restaurant. It makes an excellent accompaniment to a glass of wine. The crab topping can be prepared ahead of time but spread it only on the spring roll wrappers and bake just before serving.

1 Preheat oven to 320°F (160°C, gas 3).
2 Soften the cream cheese in a bowl with a spatula, and stir in the crabmeat and mayonnaise.
3 Mix in the dried breadcrumbs, soy sauce, salt, cayenne, and white pepper.
4 Place a spring roll wrapper on a cutting board and spread the crab/cream cheese mixture evenly with a rubber spatula.
5 Put the spring roll sheets on a cookie sheet and bake until lightly browned and crispy. Watch and turn carefully.
6 Serve on a flat bamboo basket lined with *hanshi* (Japanese writing paper; refer to Glossary).

Spring starters
Haru no otoshi
春のお通し

(from page 50)
**Udo Dressed with Plum Sauce
(Udo no Bainiku Ae)**
125 g *udo*, cannot be substituted
10 ml *su* (rice vinegar)
5 g *bainiku* (sieved flesh of salted plum), available at Japanese grocery stores
or can easily be made by sieving the salt preserved *ume boshi*.
5 g fresh wasabi
can be substituted with frozen wasabi

1 Peel *udo* with a vegetable peeler. Cut in half and soak in some water with the vinegar to remove the acid.
2 Combine all the ingredients to make the dressing.
3 Slice into 5 cm lengths, slice the piece in half lengthwise and slice the halves lengthwise into thin slices. Toss with the dressing.

**Herb Marinated Sea Bream Sashimi
(Tai no Koso Marine)**
40 g sashimi quality sea bream fillet
2 g natural sea salt
one pinch sugar
30 ml virgin olive oil
3 g lemon grass, can be substituted with any fresh herb of your choice

1 Prepare the sea bream into *san mai oroshi* cut (see page 244). Remove the skin.
2 Mix the salt and sugar well.
3 Sprinkle the filleted sea bream with the salt and sugar mixture. Let rest for 30 minutes.
4 Rinse the salt of the sea bream, pat dry and place in a dish with the olive oil and lemon grass. Marinate for 3 hours.
5 Remove the sea bream from the olive oil and slice into *sogi giri* cut (see page 247).

Miso-pickled cream cheese

Kurimu chiizu no miso zuke
クリームチーズの味噌漬け

Serves 4
1 teaspoon *mirin*
1 teaspoon *koikuchi shoyu* (soy sauce)
2 medium cloves garlic, chopped
3 1/2 oz (100 g) *moromi* miso (a soft,
brown spread of salt-pickled
vegetable mixed with unfiltered soy
sauce and miso), see Note
5 oz (125 g) cream cheese (any
generic variety of cream cheese,
e.g. Philadelphia, rather than
marscapone, works better in this
recipe as it is firmer and retains its
shape for easier slicing)
1 *baguette* (French bread), cut crosswise
into 16 slices and baked until brown
and crispy

Chinmi are unusual and luxurious delicacies that are often eaten together with *sake*. Some of these choice food items, such as exquisite sea animals or fermented seafood innards, can be a little too exotic for younger Japanese, and non-Japanese, palates. This recipe for miso-pickled cream cheese was developed for just this reason and is perfect with a chilled glass of your favorite *sake*. The inspiration for this tasty snack came from a local delicacy of Kumamoto Prefecture, tofu pickled in miso. The miso-pickled cream cheese must be prepared a week in advance.

1 In a small bowl, combine the *mirin*, soy sauce, garlic, and *moromi* miso until well mixed.
2 In a Tupperware container that comfortably fits the cream cheese, spread half of the miso mixture. Wrap the cream cheese in a cheese cloth or kitchen paper and place on top of the miso mixture. Now spread the remaining half of the mixture on top so that the cream cheese is completely covered. Refrigerate for 1 week.

3 Remove the cream cheese from the miso pickling medium and slice into 16 slices. Let it return to room temperature and serve each slice on a piece of bread.

Note: *Moromi* miso is available from Japanese grocery stores but if you are unable to locate any, use *aka* miso (red miso) softened with some *mirin*.

Sake-steamed clams

Hamaguri no saka mushi
蛤の酒蒸し

Serves 4
40 unopened clams, about 10 oz
   (300 g), thoroughly rinsed under
   running water
2/3 oz (20 g) *naga negi* (long welsh
   onion), substitute with white part of
   scallion (spring onion), finely chopped
1/4 clove garlic
1 1/2 cups (360 ml) *sake*
1/4 cup (60 ml) water
1 *taka no tsume* (dried hot red chili)
4 teaspoons *koikuchi shoyu* (soy sauce)
1 handful (5 g) *fugu negi* (welsh or
   ciboule onion stalks), substitute with
   green stalks of thin scallions (spring
   onions), finely chopped

Hamaguri, which belong to the group of venus clams, are gathered throughout Japan from winter through spring. They are delicious grilled in their shell on a charcoal fire or steamed in *sake*. We have added red chili to spice up the traditional recipe, and be sure to drink the delicious broth! *Hamaguri* can be substituted with any kind of hard clams.

1 Place all the ingredients, except for soy sauce and chopped *fugu negi*, in a saucepan and heat covered over high heat for 5 minutes.
2 Open the lid to check if all the clams have opened. If not, heat for a few more minutes. When all the clams have opened, stir in the soy sauce. Discard any clams that do not open.
3 Place the opened clams in a serving bowl with the broth, and garnish with chopped *fugu negi*.

Char-grilled Maezawa beef

Maezawa gyu no kinome miso yaki

前沢牛の木の芽味噌焼き

Serves 4
4 1/2 tablespoons *sake*
4 1/2 tablespoons *mirin*
4 teaspoons sugar
13 oz (400 g) *saikyo* miso (a sweet white miso from Kyoto), substitute with *shiro* miso (white miso)
6 1/2 oz (200 g) *shiro* miso (white miso)
13 oz (400 g) *kinome* (young *sansho* leaves), ground in a mortar and pestle (leave some whole to garnish)
12 oz (360 g) Maezawa beef tenderloin or sirloin
2 pinches natural sea salt
2 pinches freshly ground black pepper

Although Kobe beef is the most famous marbled beef from Japan, many other regions produce equally wonderful, if not better, meat such as Maezawa beef, Yonezawa, and Iga. *Kinome*, or young prickly ash leaf, is mixed with sweet miso as a flavoring for Maezawa beef in this recipe.

1 Bring *sake* and *mirin* to a boil in a saucepan boil for 1 minute to burn off the alcohol content.
2 Place both types of miso in a separate saucepan and heat over low heat, then pour in the *sake*, *mirin*, and sugar, stirring with a wooden spatula to prevent it burning. Remove from the heat and cool.
3 Stir the ground *kinome* into the cooled miso, mixing well to form a paste.

4 Skewer the beef with four skewers and sprinkle with salt and pepper. When the beef is warmed to room temperature, grill over charcoal or broil under an oven grill. Spread the paste on the browned side and grill briefly to brown, then grill the other side to your liking.
5 Slice the beef into 4 serving slices and arrange on a platter garnished with fresh *kinome* leaves.

Spanish mackerel grilled with citrus sauce

Sawara no yuzu fumi yaki

鰆の柚子風味焼き

Serves 4
1 cup plain sugar syrup
1/2 cup water
4 kinkan (kumquats)
6 1/2 tablespoons koikuchi shoyu
(soy sauce)
6 1/2 tablespoons mirin
6 1/2 tablespoons sake
Zest from 1/2 yuzu (Japanese citron),
  substitute with 1 lemon, grated
4 fillets Spanish mackerel, about 4 oz
  (120 g) each, cut in three-section fillet
  (see page 244)
8 kogomi (fiddleheads), total about 2 oz
  (60 g), blanched in salted water, then
  refreshed in cold water (optional)

Sawara, or Spanish mackerel, is caught in the Inland Sea from April to June and makes excellent grilled fish. In Kyoto, it is cured in sweet saikyo miso for one day and grilled. We have marinated it with yuzu, a fragrant Japanese citrus fruit.

1 Put 1 cup plain sugar syrup and 1/2 cup water, and the whole kumquats, in a small saucepan, and bring to a gentle boil, then simmer for 5 minutes.
2 Place soy sauce, mirin, and sake in a saucepan and heat over medium heat until it comes to a boil. Remove from heat and cool.
3 Add grated citron zest to the cooled sauce and pour over the fish, then leave to marinate for 3 or 4 hours.

4 Remove the mackerel from the marinade, skewer each slice with 2 metal or bamboo skewers (soaked in water), and grill on a charcoal grill or broil under an oven grill, taking care not to burn the fish.
5 When nicely browned on both sides and thoroughly grilled, arrange each fillet on a serving platter and garnish with poached kumquats and blanched fiddleheads.

Sea bream rice
Tai meshi
鯛飯

Serves 4
2 cups (440 g) Japanese rice, washed
  (see page 261 for washing instructions)
2 3/4 cups (700 ml) *katsuo dashi* (bonito
  stock) (see page 248)
1/2-in (5 g) very young ginger,
  peeled, cut into fine slivers and
  refreshed in water
4 teaspoons *usukuchi shoyu* (light soy
  sauce)
4 teaspoons *mirin*
1 small sea bream, about 10 oz (300 g),
  scaled, gutted, washed, and patted dry
10 *kinome* (young *sansho*) leaves

Sea bream, a spring fish that is caught mainly in the Sea of Japan and the Inland Sea, has long been considered the most important fish in Japan. Its Japanese name, *tai*, sounds like the "*tai*" in the word "*omedetai*" meaning celebratory or congratulatory, further enhancing the sea bream's image! In addition, the shimmering pinkish red color of its scales is associated with the celebratory color of red in Japan. Since it can be rather time consuming to remove the bones from this fish, you may use sea bream fillets. However, the taste will not be as rich and the presentation not as stunning.

1 Put the washed rice in a ceramic pot or a heavy-bottomed pot that will fit the sea bream comfortably. Add all the ingredients except for fish and *kinome* leaves; stir well, then heat over medium heat.
2 When it comes to a boil, lower the heat and place the sea bream on top of the rice. Simmer for about 30 minutes or until all the moisture has been absorbed into the rice.
3 Let the cooked rice sit for about 3 minutes. Garnish with fresh *kinome* leaves and serve.

Gratin of strawberries

Ichigo no guratan

苺のグラタン

Serves 4

1/2 egg + 1 egg yolk
2 tablespoons all-purpose (plain) flour
1 cup (250 ml) milk
Few drops vanilla essence
20 large strawberries, stems removed,
  halved lengthwise
1/4 cup (55 g) sugar
1 teaspoon strawberry liqueur
1 egg yolk
4 teaspoons white wine
1/2 tablespoon sugar
2 teaspoons heavy (double) cream
1 teaspoon lemon juice
2 teaspoons sugar

This dessert is not baked so it might be a bit misleading to call it a gratin, although superficially this is what it resembles. The strawberries should remain uncooked and the entire dessert should be assembled at room temperature.

1 In a mixing bowl, beat 1/2 egg and 1 egg yolk until lemon yellow, then slowly sift in the flour and continue to beat. Set aside.
2 In a saucepan, heat the milk until just boiling. Add the vanilla essence, and slowly pour the vanilla milk into the egg mixture to form a custard, stirring vigorously with a whisk so that the egg does not coagulate.
3 Pour the mixture back into the saucepan and heat over low heat until it thickens. Pour the mixture through a sieve, cool, and reserve.
4 Steep the strawberries in a bowl with the sugar and strawberry liqueur for 10 minutes.
5 In a saucepan large enough to accommodate another bowl, bring some water to a boil. Place a separate bowl in the boiling water and add the remaining 1 egg yolk. Using a whisk, beat together with the white wine, and 1/2 tablespoon sugar. When it develops a fine froth, add the heavy cream and lemon juice to form a cream sauce.
6 Spread the custard on the bottom of a gratin dish, arrange the strawberries on top, pour on the cream sauce on top, sprinkle on the remaining 2 teaspoons sugar and create a golden brown crust using a blowtorch or by broiling the dish under an oven grill.

Green tea tofu

Macha dofu

抹茶豆腐

Serves 4
1/3-oz (10-g) (5 sheets) leaf gelatin
1 stick *kanten* (4g agar-agar flakes
   or threads)
2/3 cup (50 g) powdered green tea
4 cups (1 liter) homemade soymilk
   (see page 254)
Scant 1 cup (200 g) sugar
4 black soybeans braised in syrup
   to garnish, available canned in
   Japanese grocery stores (optional)

You might want to prepare this dessert when you plan on making one of our tofu dishes; if so you can reserve some extra soymilk for this recipe. *Macha*, powered green tea used for the tea ceremony, keeps well, refrigerated, for quite some time.

1 Soak the gelatin and agar-agar together until softened.
2 Dissolve the powdered green tea with some water.
3 Place the soymilk, dissolved green tea, sugar, agar-agar, and gelatin into a saucepan and warm over medium heat. Stir the mixture continuously with a wooden spatula, scraping the bottom of the saucepan to prevent it from scorching. Remove from heat when agar-agar and gelatin are completely melted. Pour the mixture through a fine sieve and pour into a *nagashigata* (square metal mold) and chill in the refrigerator. Substitute using a square, preferably metal, box about 6 in (15 cm) square and at least 2 in (5 cm) deep but without an insert, for the *nagashigata*. When removing the finished dessert, you will have to carefully slice along the edge.
4 Slice the tofu dessert into 4 squares, garnish with black beans, and serve.

Note: If you plan on making many of our recipes, *macha* is handy to have on hand to make the summer breeze cocktail; the bicolored chestnut and green tea jellied confection; or some green tea ice cream, which is not included in this book but can be made by following any basic ice cream recipe.

Soymilk skin and strawberry millefeuille

Yuba to ichigo no mirufiyu

湯葉と苺のミルフィーユ

Serves 4
16 *yuba* (soymilk skins), approximately
  2 1/2 x 3 1/2 in (7 x 9 cm), see page 54
2 teaspoons sugar
30 large strawberries
1/4 cup (60 ml) water
1 tablespoon sugar
3/4 cup (200 ml) heavy (double) cream

You could make this dessert when you prepare one of our tofu dishes, preparing some extra soymilk for this recipe. Prepare the soymilk skin (*yuba*) by following the recipe for green bean soymilk film on page 54 but omit the green beans. Make certain that you drain off any excess soymilk from *yuba* before baking it, otherwise it will not turn crispy.

1 Preheat oven to 350°F (180°C, gas 4). Place *yuba* on a cookie sheet, a couple at a time, sprinkle with sugar, and bake for about 3 minutes. They should become nicely browned and crispy. Repeat until finished.
2 Put 18 of the strawberries, water, and sugar in a saucepan and simmer for about 30 minutes until you have made a preserve. Cool and reserve.
3 Whip the heavy cream just until it starts to form peaks. Mix in the cooled strawberry preserve.
4 Spread one sheet of *yuba* with strawberry cream, then repeat until you have 4 layers of *yuba* per serving. Garnish with remaining strawberries.

Spring blessing

Aya

礼

Makes 1 cocktail
2/3 fl oz (20 ml) fresh grapefruit juice
1/6 fl oz (5 ml) fresh lemon juice
1/2 fl oz (15 ml) vodka, chilled well in
   the freezer
2/3 fl oz (20 ml) *sakura* (cherry) liqueur,
   available in gourmet liquor stores
Few cherry blossom petals

Sakura—delicate cherry blossoms tinged in a blush of faint pink—arouse all Japanese from winter hibernation. We begin to celebrate the coming of spring with evening picnics under the blossoms, and with *sake* flowing freely throughout the evening. We are then filled with melancholy as the short-lived blossoms swirl onto the ground in the gusty winds of spring.

1 Pour the grapefruit and lemon juice through a sieve or tea strainer to remove any pulp.
2 Transfer all the ingredients, except for the petals, to a cocktail shaker and shake.
3 Pour into a cocktail glass and garnish with cherry blossom petals.

Cherry blossom and chrysanthemum leaf balls

Sakura dango to shungiku dango

桜団子と春菊団子

Serves 4

3 1/2 oz (100 g) *koshi an* (canned sweet smooth *azuki* bean paste)

3 1/2 oz (100 g) *ogura an* (canned sweet coarse *azuki* bean paste)

8 oz (250 g) *mochi* rice powder, substitute with *shiratama ko* (glutinous rice granules)

2/3 cup (150 ml) water

3 1/2 oz (100 g) *shungiku* (chrysanthemum leaves), substitute with a green leaf vegetable such as dandelion, ground in a mortar and pestle

4 oz (120 g) *sakura no hana no shio zuke* (salt-preserved cherry blossoms), soaked in several changes of water to remove the salt

1 Divide the two kinds of sweet bean paste into 1 heaped teaspoon (10 g) portions and roll into small balls, to yield 20 balls.

2 Combine the rice powder with the 2/3 cup water in a large bowl and knead thoroughly. Divide into two balls, wrap both in plastic wrap and refrigerate.

3 Mix the ground chrysanthemum leaves to one dough ball; mix the cherry blossoms to the other dough ball. Divide each into 10 portions.

4 Roll each portion into a flat circle with the palm of your hand and place a bean paste ball onto the pink dough circle and roll into a ball. Repeat with the course bean paste and the green dough.

5 Steam over medium heat for 10 minutes.

6 Arrange the balls on a platter with cherry blossom branches or skewer them with the branches. *Dango* can be served hot or at room temperature. When letting them cool, keep them covered with plastic wrap or a damp kitchen towel, as they will dry quickly.

Frozen shiso and yogurt

Kazumi

一美

Serves 4
1 tablespoon fresh grapefruit juice
1 teaspoon fresh lemon juice
5 teaspoons *shiso* (perilla) liqueur,
  substitute with plum liqueur
4 teaspoons yogurt liqueur
2 *shiso* (perilla) leaves
3/4 cup crushed ice

This frozen cocktail, ideal for warm spring evenings, is flavored with fragrant *shiso* (perilla) leaves. *Shiso* is an important herb used in many recipes as a condiment, and this is a great cocktail to make with the leftover leaves. Most Japanese grocery stores carry *shiso* leaves and they can be easily grown in a windowsill pot alongside your basil plants. You could also try making this cocktail with basil.

1 Pour the grapefruit and lemon juice through a sieve or tea strainer to remove any pulp.

2 Place all the ingredients and crushed ice into a blender and blend until smooth. Serve immediately.

summer

The backbreaking chore of scrubbing vegetables in the winter months turns to joyous splashing about in the summer. The weight of the vegetables tells us that summer is just around the corner. And it is now that we receive calls from our regular customers inquiring whether the sweetfish (*ayu*) has arrived. An increasing number of them want to celebrate the arrival of summer with a sweetfish feast. The summer evenings must be embraced with the traditional seasonal aesthetics and spirit of *iki* (enlightenment). And, in keeping with this tradition, we are perpetually masterminding presentations of coolness for the hot, humid summer evenings.

Our vegetable guru strolling through his beloved fields, nurturing his produce. The soil in the Yamazaki Farm feels warm and fluffy, and even has a wonderful clean fragrance. On one occasion, we noticed that the crops in a nearby farm were growing at a faster pace than those of the same variety in Yamazaki-san's fields. His reply to our question was "they will grow in a short while." Surely enough, his crops had outgrown those in the nearby farm when we visited his farm a few weeks later. Chemical fertilizers are capable of boosting instantaneous growth but are not capable of nurturing the natural energy contained within the plants.

Our guru, Yamazaki-san, runs the Yamazaki Farm in Mashiko County, Tochigi Prefecture. When we first encountered Yamazaki-san, his vegetables and devotion to farming moved us deeply. Here was genuine organically farmed produce. His purpose was to farm following nature's life cycle, to be rooted with nature and to abide by its laws and conditions or, to phrase it simply, to farm by the traditional methods. Yamazaki-san has enlightened us about vegetables and has nurtured in us a universal feeling for food.

The conventional image of a vegetable field is a vast lot with ridges of soil running in neat perpendicular lines planted with identical crops. Yamazaki-san's fields, however, are planted seemingly unsystematically with a confusing intermingling of different crops, withered stems of finished crop and weeds everywhere. This is neither from neglect nor from slack. By allowing such symbiosis between crops and weeds, Yamazaki-san is nurturing their potential strength to produce vigorous, healthy crops. The cucumbers and zucchinis that peek out from amongst the jungle of leaves and weeds are charged with energy and a vivacious character similar to that of the farmer himself.

The best way to eat any vegetable is to eat it as soon as it is harvested and that was the basis of our search for contract farms near Tokyo so that the vegetables could be shipped to us directly, bypassing the wholesale market distribution which adds a minimum of two days before their arrival to our kitchens. The vegetables of Yamazaki Farm are harvested and boxed personally by Yamazaki-san just before the truck departs in the morning. The wonderful fragrance of his soil fills the air when we open these boxes. The vegetables are left unwashed to maintain freshness during transportation.

The taste of Yamazaki-san's vegetables grown by traditional methods is reminiscent of the vegetables of our childhood. They have a strong flavor composed of an intertwining of sweet, bitter, tart, tangy, and spicy flavors. They also arrive in a variety of sizes and shapes, completely unlike the mass-produced vegetables of uniform size and color, which line the shelves of grocery stores. Yamazaki-san's theory is that vegetables should be harvested gradually so that we may enjoy the change in taste over a longer period of time instead of having an overabundance of the same vegetable at any one time. Our regular clients are so acquainted with these vegetables that they will comment on how large they have become. One of our popular winter dishes was inspired by a small *daikon* radish that turned up in the kitchen one day. Yamazaki-san had sent us the daikon that were thinned out from the daikon patch. These would normally be thrown out in a conventional farm for being substandard but they are delicious with a concentrated flavor and the smaller size allows us to grill them whole.

We visit frequently Yamazaki-san on the pretext of discussing the variety of crop for the next season or to pick up the vegetables for the following day. However, our real motive is to drink sake and enjoy vegetable feasts around the open fire under the kiwi pergola. Freshly pulled scallions and plucked peppers batter-fried as tempura in an iron cauldron over the fire, huge salt pickled cucumbers, new potatoes grilled with fresh basil, whole tomatoes to be bitten into, the feast continues until sunrise when Yamazaki-san returns to his fields to harvest the vegetables for us to take back.

Our relationship with Yamazaki-san has deepened such that he knows the quantities and varieties that are needed, so we almost have no need to place actual orders now. Now, he even gathers the spring mountain vegetables and the wild autumn fungus for us in the mountains and forests near his farm. As soon as this message is relayed to us by telephone, we inform dining clients about our special treat for the following evening and many of them return the following night, reserving the dish as well as the table.

below left to right Cherry tomatoes are ripened on the vine before they are shipped to Shunju where they are served as starters or half-dried to be used in our *maruyaki*, griddle cakes. The smaller *daikon*, conventionally considered sub-standard, are delicious with a concentrated flavor and the smaller size allows us to grill it whole. The zucchini blossom buds are shipped to Shunju where they are served batter-fried as tempura, but the full blooms decorate the "salon," the fire pit under the kiwi pergola where Yamazaki-san entertains his guests with vegetable feasts. *Nasu*, Japanese eggplant, is much smaller in size than Western eggplant. It is also juicier and less bitter.

Summer starter with spicy miso dip

Natsu no otoshi

夏のお通し

Serves 4
Raw salad ingredients of your choice,
  such as lettuce, radish, tomatoes,
  scallions (spring onions) etc

Spicy miso dip
1 teaspoon Korean virgin sesame oil
1/4 cup (40 g) finely chopped beef
5 tablespoons *naga negi* (long welsh
  onion), cut in thin slivers and refreshed
  in cold water (see page 251), substitute
  with white part of scallion (spring
  onion), finely minced
2 teaspoons *sake*
2 teaspoons *mirin*
2 1/2 tablespoons *shiro* miso
  (white miso)
1 2/3 tablespoons *aka* miso (red miso)
1/2 teaspoon *do ban jang* (Chinese
  fermented bean paste)
1/2 teaspoon *kochujang* (Korean
  chili paste)
2 teaspoons *katsuo dashi* (bonito stock)
  (see page 248)
1/2-in (1-cm) ginger, grated, squeezed
  to obtain juice, solids discarded

The summer starter is simply a basketful of wonderful organic vegetables that arrive daily in Shunju's kitchens from Yamazaki's farm served with a spicy meat and miso dip. You can always omit the beef from the dip if you prefer to have it meat free.

1 To make the dip, heat sesame oil in a heavy-bottomed saucepan over medium heat. Add the chopped beef and *naga negi* and sauté thoroughly.
2 When the beef changes color, add *sake*, *mirin*, white miso, and red miso in that order. Stir continuously with a wooden spatula to prevent the dip from scorching on the bottom of the pan. When the seasonings are fully incorporated with the beef, add the bean paste, chili paste, and stock and reduce the heat to low. Simmer for 20 minutes, stirring from time to time.
3 When the liquid is reduced and the dip has a thick consistency, add the ginger juice. Remove from the heat and cool.
4 Arrange raw vegetables of your choice aesthetically in a wooden bowl or handwoven basket and serve with the spicy miso dip.

Snap bean salad

Ingen salada

いんげんサラダ

Serves 4
4 cups (1 liter) water
2 tablespoons natural sea salt
10 oz (300 g) snap (French) beans,
   tops removed
2 tablespoons *dou chi jang* (Chinese
   black bean sauce with garlic)
1 teaspoon *koikuchi shoyu* (soy sauce)

Mayonnaise
10 teaspoons *wagarashi ko* (powdered
   Japanese mustard), mixed with 2 tablespoons hot water to form a paste
4 teaspoons white wine vinegar
1 egg
3/4 cup (200 ml) vegetable oil

We like to serve as many vegetables as possible in their whole form. The most important aspect of this recipe is to blanch the snap beans quickly so that they retain their raw crunchiness and to serve them with your own delicious homemade mayonnaise.

1 Bring the water and sea salt to a boil in a large saucepan over high heat and blanch the snap beans for 10–15 seconds. Drain and plunge into a bowl of iced water. When completely cooled, drain, and pat dry. Refrigerate.
2 To make the mayonnaise, mix the mustard paste with 2 teaspoons of the wine vinegar.
3 Whisk the egg in a bowl with a wire whisk until pale in color.

Continue whisking and add the mustard mixture, then very gradually whisk in 1 teaspoon of the vegetable oil. When the mixture begins to thicken and emulsify, add the remaining oil and vinegar drop by drop, alternating between each ingredient.
4 Mix the snap beans, mayonnaise, black bean sauce, and soy sauce in a bowl.

Vegetable sushi
Yasai zushi

野菜寿司

Makes 48 pieces (6 pairs x 4 servings)
2 cups (400 g) Japanese rice, washed
 and cooked (see page 260)
1 2/3 cups (400 ml) water
2 in (5 cm) *konbu* (kelp)
3/4 cup (180 ml) *su* (rice vinegar)
1/2 cup (120 ml) *sake*
1/4 cup (60 ml) *mirin*
1/3 cup (70 g) superfine (caster) sugar
2 tablespoons natural sea salt

Eggplant topping
2 *mizu nasu* (miso-pickled Japanese
 eggplants), substitute with (*nasu*)
 Japanese eggplants
1 bag *san go hachi* or *nuka* pickling
 medium, see Note

Myoga topping
8 *myoga* (mioga)
3/4 cup (180 ml) *su* (rice vinegar)
Scant 2 tablespoons superfine (castor)
 sugar
Pinch natural sea salt

Shiitake topping
3/4 cup (180 ml) *katsuo dashi* (bonito
 stock) (see page 248)
1 tablespoon *koikuchi shoyu* (soy sauce)
1 teaspoon *mirin*
8 *shiitake* mushrooms, stems removed,
 grilled until nicely browned

Turnip topping
4 small *kabu* (turnips) with leaves

Menegi topping
2 oz (60 g) *menegi* (welsh onion
 sprouts), substitute with chives
1 teaspoon Korean virgin sesame oil
Pinch natural sea salt
1 fresh wasabi, substitute with frozen
 fresh or tube wasabi

Yamagobo topping
16 *mitsuba* (Japanese wild chervil)
2 2/3 oz (80 g) soy-pickled *yamagobo*
 (substitute with miso-pickled *yamagobo*)

Although sushi is recognized internationally as a cuisine with lavish use of raw seafood, vegetable and pickled vegetable sushi have been introduced in some exclusive sushi restaurants as a singular signature piece. Vegetables being a central theme for Shunju cuisine, we have assorted different types of summer vegetables and pickles to create one dish. (One portion of sushi is always served in pairs.)

Eggplant topping
Lightly rub *mizu nasu* with sea salt and leave, covered, for about 20 minutes to prevent discoloration. Pickle whole in *san go hachi* or *nuka* medium for 8 hours (see Note). Slice the pickled eggplant into 1/4-in (5-mm) slices.

Myoga topping
Blanch *myoga* in boiling water for 30 seconds. Drain and reserve. Boil rice vinegar, sugar, and salt in a saucepan to boiling point, remove from heat, add *myoga* and cool. Marinate for 3 hours.

Shiitake topping
Combine stock, soy sauce, and *mirin*. Marinate grilled *shiitake* in the sauce for 10 minutes. Wipe off excess marinade and reserve.

Turnip topping
Slice turnips (with leaves) into 1/2-in (1-cm) slices; the leaf section should be about 3/4 in (2 cm) long. Sprinkle with sea salt and leave for about 10 minutes until softened.

Menegi topping
Cut the roots off the *menegi* taking care to leave them aligned, and drizzle with sesame oil and sea salt

shortly before arranging them on top of *nigiri*.

Yamagobo topping
Blanch *mitsuba* for 10 seconds, plunge into cold water, drain and reserve. Cut off the leaves and hold two together and straighten. Cut the pickled *yamagobo* into 2-in (5-cm) lengths. Arrange on top of *nigiri* and tie with the blanched *mitsuba*.

Sushi rice
While the rice is cooking, boil *sake*, *mirin*, castor sugar, and sea salt to boiling point. Remove from heat and cool. Add rice vinegar and *konbu* to cooled mixture. Remove *konbu* after 10 minutes. For preparation of the sushi rice and assembling each piece of sushi, refer to page 250. Assemble at once all the other ingredients to prevent the rice from drying.

Note: *Nuka* pickling medium can be substituted with the following solution: mix 1 1/2 cups (360 ml) water with 2 teaspoons natural sea salt, 1 teaspoon *konbu cha* and 1 in (3 cm) of *konbu*. Soak eggplant for 1 hour.

Miniature eggplants and shoots in jellied consommé

Ko nasu to junsai no reisei yose

小茄子とじゅんさいの冷製寄せ

Serves 4

16 *ko nasu* (miniature eggplants), substitute with the smallest *nasu* (Japanese eggplants) you can find
4 oz (120 g) fresh or bottled *junsai* (water shield shoots)
Vegetable oil
1 teaspoon natural sea salt
Pinch black pepper
4 teaspoons *usukuchi shoyu* (light soy sauce)
1 tablespoon *mirin*
1 1/3 cups (340 ml) *katsuo dashi* (bonito stock) (see page 248)
1/4 cup (60 ml) chicken stock
1/2 oz (15 g) sheet gelatin, soaked until softened
1 in (2 1/2 cm) ginger, grated, squeezed to obtain juice, solids discarded
7 teaspoons fresh wasabi, substitute with frozen fresh or tube wasabi

Nasu, or eggplant, is perhaps the most popular of all the summer vegetables; there are currently about 30 varieties of eggplants cultivated in Japan, and they come in every shape and size. All Japanese eggplants are much less bitter than their Western counterparts and do not need to be salted before cooking. These miniature eggplants make a beautiful presentation as they are used whole and nestled in an amber jelly together with *junsai*, another summer delicacy. Try to serve this dish in glassware, whether in one large bowl or smaller individual bowls.

1 Remove the stems from the eggplants and cut 6 vertical stripes about 2 mm deep.
2 Blanch the *junsai*, refresh in cold water, drain and reserve. Try not to lose its gelatinous coating. If using bottled *junsai*, there is no need to blanch it.
3 Pour vegetable oil into a pan until it reaches about 2 in (5 cm) in depth. Heat to 350°F (180°C) and lightly deep-fry the eggplants.
4 Remove eggplants, plunge into boiling water to remove the oil, then lift out with a slotted spoon and transfer to a clean saucepan. Add in the sea salt, black pepper, light soy sauce, *mirin*, and bonito and chicken stock and heat over medium heat until it reaches boiling point. Lower the heat and simmer for 2–3 minutes. Remove eggplants with the slotted spoon and reserve.
5 Reheat the stock to boiling point, remove from heat and add the softened gelatin, stirring with a spatula. When the gelatin is thoroughly dissolved, add the ginger juice. Pour into a bowl set in a larger bowl filled with iced water. When the gelatin and stock mixture starts to thicken, add *junsai*.
6 Arrange the cooled eggplants in one large glass bowl or small individual glass bowls and pour the chilled gelatin mixture on top. Cover with plastic wrap to prevent it from drying out, and chill overnight in the refrigerator. Garnish with grated wasabi.

Sweetfish grilled with sea salt

Ayu no shio yaki
鮎の塩焼き

Serves 4
4 *ayu* (sweetfish), substituted with small trout, rinsed, and patted dry
3 1/2 oz (100 g) natural sea salt
4 sprigs *tade* (water pepper; for presentation only, so substitute with any elegant sprigs)
2 *sudachi* (small acidic citrus fruit), halved, substitute with lemon wedges

1 Skewer sweetfish with a metal skewer (entering through its mouth and exiting just before the dorsal fin). Pat some salt on the tail, pelvic, and dorsal fins.
2 Charcoal grill or broil under an oven grill until cooked. It can also be baked in a 482°F (250°C, gas 10) oven for 10–15 minutes but brown briefly under a broiler to finish. Serve with *sudachi* halves (or lemon wedges).

Skewer-grilled rice-stuffed sweetfish

Ayu meshi no kushi yaki
鮎飯の串焼き

Serves 4
4 *ayu* (sweetfish), about 6 1/2 oz (200 g) each, air-cured overnight (*ichiyaboshi*, see page 252), substitute with small trout
1 1/4 oz (40 g) *kabu* (Japanese turnip) greens, minced and pressed with sea salt, excess moisture squeezed out
4 *shiso* (perilla) leaves, minced
4 teaspoons white sesame seeds, toasted until golden brown
2 2/3 cups (400 g) cold cooked rice

Tade sauce
1/4 cup (50 g) rice
1 cup (250 ml) water
3/4 cup (200 ml) *tade su*, see Note

Kimo sauce
Sweetfish entrails
Pinch natural sea salt
2 1/2 tablespoons Korean virgin sesame oil

1 Butterfly the sweetfish and air cure overnight. Reserve the entrails for making the *kimo* sauce.
2 To make the *tade* sauce, first prepare a rice porridge by simmering washed rice and water in a saucepan for about 30 minutes. Cool, then combine with the *tade su* in a mortar and purée with a pestle to make *tade* sauce. Set aside.
3 To make the *kimo* sauce, bake the sweetfish entrails in a 350°F (180°C, gas 4) oven for 3 minutes. Then remove and mince on a cutting board with a pinch of sea salt and mix in the sesame oil. Set aside.

4 Mix turnip greens, *shiso* leaves, sesame seeds, and cold rice in a bowl. Divide into 4 portions and press evenly onto sweetfish, skin side down. Fold the fish back to its original form and skewer with two bamboo sticks.
5 Serve with *tade* sauce and *kimo* sauce.

Note: *Tade su* is made by steeping pounded water pepper leaves and buds in rice vinegar but is widely available bottled from Japanese foodstores.

Sweetfish fried with river algae

Ayu no kawa nori age

鮎の川のり揚げ

Serves 4

4 *ayu* (sweetfish), air-cured overnight (see page 252), substitute with small trout
8 sheets *kawa nori* (dried river algae), substitute with *ao nori* (green *nori*), minced
Vegetable oil
1 cup (100 g) all-purpose (plain) flour
1/3 cup (40 g) *katakuri* starch (from Japanese dog's tooth violet), substitute with potato or cornstarch
4 *sudachi* (small acidic citrus fruit), halved, substitute with lemon wedges

Sweetfish has a very delicate, light flavor and it is delicious deep-fried in a thin coating of flour. However, it also tastes great deep-fried with a tempura batter. *Kawa nori* is a species of algae which grows on rocks in mountain streams and these two delicacies, which the river blesses us with in the summer, compliment one another perfectly.

1 Butterfly fillet the sweetfish and air-cure overnight (see page 252). Press minced *kawa nori* evenly on the sweetfish before air-curing.
2 Pour vegetable oil in a pan until it reaches 6 in (15 cm) in depth. Heat to 325°F (160°C).
3 Sift the flour and *katakuri* (or other) starch together. Coat the sweetfish in the flour mixture, then deep-fry the fish until nicely browned.
4 Remove with a slotted spoon and drain on paper towel. Cut into three pieces and serve with *sudachi* halves (or lemon wedges).

Chilled sweetfish and rice soup

Ayu no ryohan

鮎の涼飯

Serves 4

2/3 medium *nasu* (Japanese eggplant), about 1 1/2 oz (50 g)

1/2 *kyuri* (Japanese cucumber), very thinly sliced

2 3/4 oz (80 g) *kabu* (Japanese turnip), with leaves cut to 1/2 in (1 cm), peeled and thinly sliced lengthwise

1 1/4 oz (40 g) *myoga* (mioga), cut in thin slivers (see page 251)

8 *shiso* (perilla) leaves, cut in thin slivers (see page 251)

1 tablespoon natural sea salt

2 cups (500 ml) water

2 *ayu* (sweetfish), substitute with small trout, butterflied (see page 252)

2 3/4 cups (720 ml) *katsuo dashi* (bonito stock) (see page 248)

1 tablespoon *usukuchi shoyu* (light soy sauce)

1 tablespoon *mirin*

2 heaped cups (320 g) cold cooked rice

2 teaspoons white sesame seeds, toasted until golden brown, to garnish

During the long, hot summer months, we often make *mizu chazuke*, the chilled summer version of the favorite *chazuke*, rice covered with hot tea or *katsuo dashi*, to nourish our body and soul when we have no appetite. You can make this dish using any small river fish, or even with no fish at all and just with the vegetables.

1 Half the eggplant and slice lengthwise very thinly. Wash all the sliced vegetables lightly in a colander. Dissolve 1 tablespoon sea salt in 2 cups water and soak the vegetables until softened, about 30 minutes .

2 Preheat oven to 356°F (180°C, gas 4). Wash the fish under cold running water, pat dry, and sprinkle lightly with sea salt. Grill or broil until nicely browned, about 7 minutes. When cool, remove the head, bones, fins, and entrails from the fish and shred the flesh with your fingers. Set aside.

3 Heat bonito stock, soy sauce, and *mirin* in a saucepan over medium high heat until boiling. Remove from heat and set the pot in a large bowl filled with iced water and cool.

4 Wash the rice lightly in a colander with cold running water. Drain well and place in a serving bowl. Tightly squeeze the water from the sliced vegetables, then arrange on top of the rice. Arrange the shredded fish on top of the vegetables.

5 Taste and correct bonito stock mixture for salt. Pour into the bowl from the side of the rice, taking care not to disturb the arranged toppings. Sprinkle sesame seeds on top and serve.

Fresh basket tofu

Zaru dofu

ざる豆腐

Serves 4

1 2/3 cups (400 ml) homemade soymilk, (see page 254)

2 teaspoons natural *nigari* (bittern, see Note on page 53)

Condiments

5 g *banno negi*, finely sliced, substitute with fine scallions (sping onions)

5 g *zha cai* (Sichuan vegetable), minced (available from Chinese supermarkets)

Shiro shoyu (white soy sauce), substitute with *usukuchi shoyu* (light soy sauce)

1/4 cup *ito gaki* (extra thin bonito shavings)

2 1/4 teaspoons *aka* miso (red miso)

1/3 clove garlic, grated

Originally, tofu shops drained freshly made tofu in baskets before molding it into blocks in wooden vats. Recently, this shapeless basket tofu has become very popular and it is now shipped to restaurants overnight from tofu shops across Japan. However, once you've mastered a few simple techniques, tofu is quite easy to make and we think that this fresh, homemade version is well worth the effort. When you use our recipe for making soymilk, the tofu is so rich and sweet that you'll want to eat it without any sauce or condiments. But, if you do want soy sauce, use white soy sauce or natural sea salt so it doesn't stain the beautiful tofu.

1 Place the *banno negi*, Sichuan vegetable, soy sauce, and bonito shavings in separate bowls.

2 Combine the miso and garlic, and place in a bowl. Set aside.

3 Prepare the basic soymilk recipe (page 254) by following steps 1 through 8.

4 Pour the soymilk into saucepan, heat over low heat stirring with a wooden or bamboo spatula scraping the bottom to prevent from scorching. When the temperature reaches 167°F (75°C), normally after about 7 or 8 minutes, turn off the heat. Pour in the *nigari* and stir with a wooden or bamboo spoon.

5 Line a round bamboo basket, about 4 in (10 cm) deep and 6 in (15 cm) in diameter, with a square of cheesecloth large enough to extend over the edge of the basket. Pour the soymilk into the basket

6 When the soymilk has cooled to room temperature and become firm, chill in the refrigerator (still in the basket) to about 41°F (5°C).

7 Gently remove the tofu by lifting the cheesecloth. Carefully flip the tofu over in your hands or on a plate and place it back into the basket the other way up (with the smooth side, the side that was originally underneath, on top). Serve with the condiments.

Fresh bamboo tofu
Take dofu
竹豆腐

Serves 4
Bamboo tofu
3 1/4 cups (800 ml) homemade soymilk (see page 254)
1 tablespoon natural *nigari* (bittern, see Note on page 53)

Green bean bamboo tofu
3 1/4 cups (800 ml) homemade soymilk (see page 254)
Pinch natural sea salt
9 oz (280 g) *endomame* (shelled green peas), substitute with *edamame* (podded green soybeans) or *soramame* (fava/broad beans)

Sesame bamboo tofu
3 1/4 cups (800 ml) homemade soymilk (see page 254)
1 heaped teaspoon black sesame seeds, toasted and finely ground with a mortar and pestle

Condiments
40 g *shiso* (perilla) leaves, cut in thin slivers (see page 251) and refreshed in cold water for 10 minutes
2 3/4 oz (80 g) *naga negi* (long welsh onion), cut in thin slivers (see page 251) and refreshed in cold water, substitute with white part of scallion (spring onion)
4 3x3-in (7x7-cm) bamboo containers
Koikuchi shoyu (soy sauce)

Take or bamboo plays an important role in Japanese culture. Not only does it provide us with beautiful forests but also with an important architectural material for fences, ceilings, floors, and decorative elements in the garden. At Shunju, we even make our own bamboo dishware including chopsticks, *sake* containers, dishes, and, of course, our *take dofu* containers. Try any of these three bamboo tofu recipes (using wooden containers if bamboo containers are not available) and serve with the condiments.

Bamboo tofu
1 Prepare the basic soymilk recipe (page 254) by following steps 1 through 8. Pour the soymilk into a saucepan and heat over medium heat, stirring with a wooden or bamboo spatula to prevent it from burning.
2 When the soymilk reaches 140°F (60°C), pour it into the four bamboo containers, add *nigari* and stir quickly. Stop stirring once the soymilk starts to coagulate. Chill.
3 For the condiments, combine *shiso* leaves and *negi* slivers in a small dish and serve together with soy sauce.

Green bean bamboo tofu
1 Prepare the basic soymilk recipe (page 254) by following steps 1 through 8.
2 Boil water in a saucepan with a pinch of sea salt over high heat and cook the shelled green peas until tender.

3 Blend the soymilk and boiled peas until the peas are finely ground. Pass the mixture through a fine sieve and mash any remaining bits.
4 Pour the mixture into a pot and follow the above instructions for bamboo tofu starting from step 2.
5 For the condiments, combine *shiso* leaves and *negi* slivers in a small dish and serve together with soy sauce.

Sesame bamboo tofu
1 Prepare the basic soymilk recipe (page 254) for following steps 1 through 8.
2 Pour the soymilk and ground black sesame into a pot and follow the above instructions for bamboo tofu starting from step 2.
3 For the condiments, combine *shiso* leaves and *negi* slivers in a small dish and serve together with soy sauce.

Kelp marinated sea bass

Suzuki no kobu jime

鱸の昆布〆

Serves 4

3 1/2 oz (100 g) *suzuki* (sea bass)
Pinch natural sea salt
2 pieces *konbu* (kelp), each 8 in (20 cm) in length
2 *myoga* (mioga), cut into needle-thin slivers and refreshed in cold water (see page 251)
6 *hana hojiso*, substitute with *shiso* (perilla) leaves in *sengiri* cut, see page 251
1 fresh wasabi (root), substitute with frozen fresh or tube wasabi
Koikuchi shoyu (soy sauce)

As with yellowtail and striped (grey) mullet, sea bass is known as a *shusse* (career promotion) fish since it is given different names at the various stages of its life: *kayakari*, as a young fish; *seigo*, when it reaches 11 in (25 cm) in length, normally as a one-year-old; *fukko*, when it reaches 12 in (30 cm) in length, normally after two to three years; and finally *suzuki*, when it reaches 24 in (60 cm) in length, normally at four or five years of age. Marinating raw fish in *konbu* (kelp) has two purposes: one is to enhance its flavor, as *konbu* is the richest known source of natural monosodium glutamate (MSG), and the other is to preserve the fish for an extra day. Sea bass, being a very large and expensive fish, is normally eaten as sashimi or *arai* (water refreshed sashimi), on the first day, and enjoyed as *kobu jime* on the second day.

1 Cut the sea bass into two fillets, removing the pelvic bone (see page 244). Sprinkle lightly with sea salt and set aside.
2 Lightly wipe the *konbu* sheets with a clean damp cloth or paper towel to remove any grit but take care not to wipe off the flavorful white powder on the kelp surface.
3 Sandwich both sea bass fillets between two pieces of *konbu* and wrap with plastic wrap. Refrigerate for half a day.
4 Unwrap and place the used *konbu* on a serving platter. Cut the fillets into *sogi giri* cut (see page 247) and arrange on the *konbu*. Serve with *myoga*, *hana hojiso* leaves, grated wasabi, and soy sauce.

Chilled green soybean soup

Edamame no surinagashi

枝豆のすり流し

Serves 4
3 1/3 tablespoons *mirin*
4 cups (1 liter) water
2 tablespoons natural sea salt
3 cups (300 g) *edamame* (podded green
   soybeans), substitute with *soramame*
   (fava/broad beans) or *endomame*
   (shelled green peas)
3/4 cup (200 ml) *katsuo dashi* (bonito
   stock) (see page 248)
1 teaspoon sugar
3 1/3 tablespoons milk
Pinch natural sea salt
4 sprigs chervil

During the long, hot summer months, we often make *surinagashi*, a chilled summer soup of puréed vegetables. It can be served as an appetizer or as an in-between course to cleanse the palate.

1 Put *mirin* in a saucepan and boil off the alcohol content to leave about 2 tablespoons. Cool and reserve.
2 Bring the water and sea salt to a boil in a large pot of water over high heat and boil soybeans for 5 minutes. Drain and plunge into a bowl of iced water. When completely cooled, drain and pat dry.
3 Pop soybeans out of the pod, then peel the thin skin off the beans.
4 Set 4 beans aside to garnish, then purée the remainder in a blender with the stock. Add *mirin*, sugar, and milk and continue to blend. Pass the mixture through a fine sieve and mash any remaining bits. Taste and add salt if necessary. Chill.
5 Pour chilled soup into cups and float one soybean and a sprig of chervil in each.

Octopus sashimi

Ike dako no butsu giri

活だこのぶつ切り

Serves 4

9 oz (280 g) fresh octopus leg, briefly blanched to sterilize it, substitute with frozen, boiled octopus leg
Handful natural sea salt
2 quarts (2 liters) water
1 cup (30 g) green tea leaves
4 teaspoons Korean virgin sesame oil
1 1/2 tablespoons white sesame seeds
Pinch natural sea salt
40 pine nuts
20 Korean red chili pepper threads

Although we refer to this dish as sashimi, octopus is almost always boiled and never served raw except in very rare cases when it is served alive. Despite its scary appearance which has made it an unfamiliar seafood in most Western diets, it has a clean, subtle taste which appeals to all lovers of shellfish. Octopus is normally served with sea salt and a squeeze of *sudachi*, but we have tossed it with our wonderful Korean virgin sesame oil.

1 Put the octopus leg in a bowl and sprinkle generously with sea salt. Hold the leg firmly with one hand and rub on the salt briskly with the other. After a few minutes, thin white foam will gradually appear. Wash the slippery foam off thoroughly under cold running water.
2 Bring 2 quarts water to a boil and add the green tea. Boil for 1 minute. Drain through a colander to remove the tea leaves, and boil again. When the water reaches a full boil, blanch the octopus for 20 seconds, then drain.
3 Cut the octopus into 3/4-in (2-cm) pieces by cutting diagonally across the leg and turning it after each cut. Toss in a bowl with sesame oil, sesame seeds, sea salt, and pine nuts. Arrange on a serving dish. Garnish with red pepper threads.

Sake-steamed abalone

Awabi no saka mushi

鮑の酒蒸し

Serves 4
1 1-lb (500-g) abalone with shell
6 1/2 oz (200 g) fresh seaweed
(*wakame*), cut into 1 1/2-in (4-cm)
lengths, substitute with dried seaweed
(reconstitute in cold water for several
minutes) or salt preserved seaweed
(soak in cold water for 1 hour, then
quickly blanch)
4 cups (1 liter) water
1 teaspoon natural sea salt
4 oz (120 g) *daikon*, cut in 1/2 in (1-cm)
slices, optional
7 tablespoons *sake*

Most shellfish reach their prime in late spring, but abalone only reaches maturity in the summer, making it a truly summer shellfish. There are two species of abalone in Japan, one with yellow tinted meat which is softer and more suited for steaming or braising, another with blue tinted meat which is firmer and more suited for a kind of sashimi called *mizu gai*, chilled in iced water to further emphasize its crunchiness. *Sake* and *daikon* both tenderize the abalone in this recipe.

1 Remove abalone meat from its shell and prepare according to the steps on page 249. Reserve the liver to make fragrant abalone liver (see below).
2 Place abalone meat in a saucepan with water, sea salt, *daikon*, and half of the *sake*. Heat over high heat until boiling, then lower the heat to low and simmer for 2 hours.
3 Place a steamer, large enough to accommodate a shallow bowl containing abalone and seaweed, over high heat until steam starts to rise.

4 Arrange seaweed in a shallow bowl, place the braised abalone on top, and sprinkle with remaining *sake*. Steam over high heat for 10 minutes.
5 Remove the bowl from the steamer, slice the piping hot abalone diagonally, and return it to its shell. Either serve in the shallow bowl (used for steaming) together with the hot soup, or arrange the seaweed on a large platter, place the abalone shell on top and serve the soup in *sake* cups. Serve hot or at room temperature.

Fragrant abalone liver

Awabi no kimo shiokara

鮑の肝塩辛

Serves 4
2 2/3 oz (80 g) abalone liver
1 clove garlic garlic, peeled and grated
2 teaspoons Korean virgin sesame oil
2 teaspoons *koikuchi shoyu* (soy sauce)
Pinch Korean large red chili pepper flakes

1 Purée the abalone liver by mincing it on the cutting board with a knife.
2 Mix the puréed liver with the garlic and all the seasonings. Let stand for 1 hour before serving (at room temperature).

Flounder carpaccio

Karei no karuppacho

鰈のカルパッチヨ

Serves 4
1 medium tomato
13 oz (400 g) flounder fillets, see
  page 246
Natural sea salt
Coarsely ground white pepper
1/2 teaspoon minced fresh dill
1/2 teaspoon minced fresh Italian
  parsley
Juice of 1/2 lemon
2 tablespoons extra virgin olive oil
20 sprigs fresh tarragon
20 sprigs fresh dill
20 sprigs fresh chervil

You can substitute flounder with other firm fleshed white fish, but be certain that the fish is perfectly fresh. The quality of the raw fish and olive oil will determine the outcome of this recipe. Chill your serving platter before plating this dish.

1 Immerse the tomato in boiling water for 5 seconds, then plunge it immediately into iced water, drain and skin. Cut the tomato in half, remove the seeds and dice into 5-mm cubes.
2 Prepare the flounder fillets into *sogi giri* cut (page 247). Arrange in a circular pattern on a platter.

3 Sprinkle sea salt and freshly ground white pepper on the flounder slices.
4 Evenly distribute the diced tomato on the fish, then sprinkle on minced dill and parsley.
5 Pour the lemon juice and olive oil, and garnish with fresh tarragon, dill and chervil leaves.

Warm lettuce salad

On retasu salada

温レタスサラダ

Serves 4
3 1/2 quarts (3 1/2 liters) water
Pinch natural sea salt
1 iceberg lettuce, about 1 lb (500 g),
  wilted leaves discarded, cut in
  half vertically, and washed under
  running water
4 tablespoons sesame oil
2 tablespoons vegetable oil
2 cloves garlic, peeled and minced
1 oz (30 g) bacon, minced
1 oz (30 g) *takana* pickles, minced
1 tablespoon *sake*
2 tablespoons *koikuchi shoyu*
  (soy sauce)
Pinch freshly ground black pepper

Iceberg lettuce is generally considered a bland, unappealing vegetable, but the organically grown summer lettuce from Yamazaki-san's fields and from the highlands near the Japanese Alps is wonderfully crispy and juicy. Blanching this lettuce brings out the juiciness and a beautiful shade of green. This is a very simple dish to prepare but you must work very quickly, so all ingredients should be measure and prepared beforehand.

1 In a pot large enough to hold the two lettuce halves, bring the water and salt to a boil. Blanch the lettuce for 20 seconds, stirring continuously. Drain in a colander.
2 Cut off the stem of the hot lettuce and cut each half into 4 equal sections. Arrange in serving bowl.
3 Heat the sesame and vegetable oils over high heat in a wok. Fry the garlic until it gives off a fragrant aroma, then add the bacon and then the *takana* pickles. Stir continuously so that none of the ingredients burn. When the bacon has browned, add *sake*, soy sauce, and pepper, and pour the hot dressing onto the lettuce.

Fruit tomato tempura

Frutsu tomato no tempura

フルーツトマトの天ぷら

Serves 4
2 eggs
1/2 cup (120 ml) iced water
1 cup (120 g) all-purpose (plain) flour,
 sifted and refrigerated
12 fresh basil leaves, roughly torn
 (plus extra, whole, to garnish)
Vegetable oil
4 fruit tomatoes, substitute with small,
 firm vine-ripened tomatoes
1/3 cup (80 ml) fresh cream
1 1/3 oc (40 g) hard cheese such as
 Gouda
1/3 oz (10 g) blue cheese such as
 Roquefort (use only the white part,
 not the mold)
4 pinches natural sea salt

As cooking increases a tomato's acidity, this recipe uses the sweeter fruit tomato but even then, it should be deep-fried very quickly. The fruit tomato is a newly developed tomato hybrid which has a reduced water content and, consequently, a greater level of sweetness. At 2 1/2–3 1/2 oz (70–100 g), it is smaller and firmer than most tomatoes.

1 Beat the eggs and iced water in a bowl, then add the flour and torn basil. Stir briefly with thick chopsticks. Do not mix to a smooth batter as tempura batter should always contain lumps of flour.
2 Pour vegetable oil in a saucepan until it reaches 6 in (15 cm) in depth. Heat to 374°F (190°C).
3 Dip a whole, unpeeled tomato in the batter and deep-fry for 1 1/2 minutes; overcooking the tomato causes it to become acidic. Make sure that you maintain the temperature of the oil at 374°F (190°C). Remove the tomato with a slotted spoon and drain on a rack. Repeat with remaining tomatoes.
4 Melt the cream and two kinds of cheese in a microwave oven or over low heat. Season with natural sea salt. Spread the cheese cream sauce on a plate, place the fried tomato in the middle, and garnish with whole basil leaves.

Chilled braised winter melon with crab sauce

Togan no kani ankake

冬瓜の蟹あんかけ

Serves 4
11 oz (320 g) *togan* (wax gourd/winter melon), cut in 2 1/2-in (6-cm) squares, peeled
2 quarts (2 liters) water
4 cups (1 liter) *katsuo dashi* (bonito stock) (see page 248)
2 1/2 tablespoons *mirin*
2 1/2 tablespoons *usukuchi shoyu* (light soy sauce)
Pinch natural sea salt
1 oz (30 g) *menegi* (welsh onion sprouts), substitute with chives

Crab sauce
1 1/4 cups (300 ml) *katsuo dashi* (bonito stock) (see page 248)
2 teaspoons *mirin*
2 teaspoons *usukuchi shoyu* (light soy sauce)
1/2 cup (60 g) king or snow crabmeat
1 egg, beaten
3 tablespoons *katakuri* starch, substitute with potato starch
2 tablespoons water
Pinch natural sea salt

Togan, known as wax gourd or winter melon in English, originates from Southeast Asia but it is historically a popular summer vegetable in Japan. It has a very high water content and is said to lower the body temperature. This dish was inspired by a Chinese dish which uses the gourd as a case in which to steam the soup. We use the case raw as the green color is more beautiful, but it may be steamed and eaten if you like.

1 To prepare the crab sauce, bring the bonito stock, *mirin*, and soy sauce to a boil over high heat. When it reaches a boil, lower the heat to medium and add the crabmeat. Skim off the foam that rises to the surface. Slowly pour in the beaten egg in a fine stream in a circular motion so that it becomes fluffy. Dissolve the starch in 2 tablespoons water and stir in a little at a time, checking the thickness so that it does not become clumpy or too thick. Remove from the heat and set aside to cool.
2 To prepare the gourd, bring the water to a boil and boil the gourd until it is easily pierced with a bamboo skewer or fork, about 5 minutes. Drain in a colander and cool in iced water.

3 Bring bonito stock, *mirin*, and soy sauce to a boil over high heat. Add the gourd and, when it returns to a boil, lower the heat to low and simmer for 10 minutes. Taste and add more salt if necessary. Remove from the heat and set the pot in a large bowl filled with iced water and cool.
4 Arrange gourd on a platter and cover with the sauce. Garnish with the welsh onion sprouts.

Note: As *togan* is very large, we often serve the dish in the hollowed gourd. Slice off the top, about 8-in (20-cm) down, then cut a smaller slice off the bottom to enable it to stand. Scoop out the seeds and pulp. Alternatively, slice the whole gourd in half and make two serving dishes.

Blanched pike conger with green dressing

Hamo no yubiki midori sauce

鱧の湯引き緑ソース

Serves 4
6 1/2 oz (200 g) *hamo* (pike conger)
4 cups (1 liter) water
2 tablespoons *sake*
3 *tade* (water pepper) leaves, for
  decoration not taste, substitute with
  tarragon leaves

Green dressing
1/3 cup (90 ml) *tade su* (see Note
  page 102)
2 teaspoons superfine (castor) sugar
Pinch natural sea salt
Pinch white pepper
2 tablespoons extra virgin olive oil

Vinegar-pickled *myoga*
1/4 cup (50 g) superfine (castor) sugar
Pinch natural sea salt
Scant 1/2 cup (100 ml) vinegar
2 cups (500 ml) water
4 *myoga* (mioga)
Pinch natural sea salt

Hamo, or pike conger, is a summer delicacy caught in the Inland Sea. It has a large number of bones which must be finely cut with a special knife known as *honegiri bocho*. Pike conger is normally served with sieved salted plum but we are pairing it with the refreshing taste of water pepper (*tade*), a willow-like herb translated as "nettle" in the title of Junichiro Tanizaki's book *Some Prefer Nettles*. Although the texture of pike conger cannot be substituted, this sauce works very well with any blanched sashimi-quality, white-fleshed fish.

1 Place the fish on a cutting board and cut off its head. Insert the tip of your knife at the head end and make a shallow incision along the dorsal fin keeping the blade flat. Insert the knife deeper until you can feel the backbone against the blade. Cut through the head to butterfly fillet the fish. Remove the backbone, gills, and entrails.
2 If the butterfly fillet is more than 3 in (7–8 cm) wide, place the fillet skin side down and trim off the edges from both sides.
3 Place on the cutting board with its tail to the left, skin side down. Holding the flesh down firmly with your left hand, slice crosswise firmly with one stroke with a *honegiri* knife, starting at the right side of the fillet. Make certain that you do not cut the skin, and break the flesh. You should only be cutting through the fine bones. Repeat the procedure. The cut should be about 2 mm apart. When you have continued the cutting up to its tail, the flesh should be held together only by its skin. Cut into 1 1/4-in (3-cm) lengths.

4 Bring the water and *sake* to a boil in a saucepan over medium high heat. Lower the heat and, using a slotted ladle, blanch each fish piece separately by carefully lowering the ladle into the water 2 or 3 times, and immediately plunging it into iced water. Repeat until all the fish is blanched.
5 Prepare the dressing by mixing *tade su*, sugar, salt, and pepper in a bowl and whisking in the olive oil.
6 To prepare the vinegar-pickled mioga, first bring the sugar, salt, vinegar, and 1/3 cup (100 ml) of the water to a boil, then remove from the heat. Cool and set aside in an airtight plastic container. Bring the remaining 1 2/3 cups (400 ml) of water to a boil with the salt, and blanch the mioga for about 20 seconds. Drain and marinate in the reserved vinegar sauce in the refrigerator. When ready to serve, remove the mioga and slice lengthwise.
7 Pat each piece of pike dry. Arrange in the center of a serving dish and pour the dressing around the fish. Garnish with water pepper leaves and pickled *myoga* slices.

Warm zucchini and beef salad

Zukkini to gyuniku no salada

ズッキーニと牛肉のサラダ

Serves 4

4 small yellow and green zucchinis
  (courgettes), washed thoroughly
4 cups (1 liter) water
1 heaped tablespoon natural sea salt
4 teaspoons extra virgin olive oil
10 oz (300 g) beef tenderloin (one piece)
Pinch natural sea salt
Pinch cracked black pepper
2 teaspoons vegetable oil
2 teaspoons cognac
1 tablespoon butter, softened to room
  temperature
2 teaspoons *koikuchi shoyu* (soy sauce)
1/4 lemon

The beautiful green and yellow zucchinis from Yamazaki-san's fields are the inspiration for this dish. It is very important that you use a good quality extra virgin olive oil in order to keep this dish light and to not overpower the delicate taste of the zucchini.

1 Peel and halve the zucchinis lengthwise, then remove the seeds and slice lengthwise into long, pasta-like 1/4-in (5-mm) square strips.
2 Bring the water and salt to a boil and blanch the zucchini for 10 seconds. Drain in a colander and toss in a bowl with olive oil while it is still piping hot.
3 Cut the beef into roughly 2-in (5-cm) widths, then cut in very thin slices, and season with salt and pepper.
4 Heat oil in a skillet and briefly sauté the beef slices, then flambé with cognac and add the butter.
5 Arrange the zucchini strips on a platter and top with beef slices. Mix the remaining meat juices in the pan with soy sauce and pour the hot dressing on top. Serve with the lemon wedge.

Bird's nest salad

Sugomori salada
巣ごもりサラダ

Serves 4
3 1/2 oz (100 g) pumpkin
3 oz (80 g) iceberg lettuce
3 oz (80 g) carrot
3 oz (80 g) *kyuri* (Japanese cucumber),
   substituted with deseeded Western
   cucumber
3 oz (80 g) *nagaimo* (Japanese yam)
4 *shiso* (perilla) leaves
4 *myoga* (mioga)
Vegetable oil
1/3 cup (80 ml) *ponzu*, see page 57
4 egg yolks

Apart from the crispy pumpkin slivers, *shiso* leaves, and *ponzu* dressing, the choice of remaining vegetables is largely your own and there is much room for improvization.

1 Cut all the vegetables into needle thin slivers, refresh in cold water, and drain before use (see page 251).
2 Heat 2 in (5 cm) oil in a pan until 356°F (180°C) and deep-fry pumpkin slivers until lightly browned and crispy, about 20 seconds. Remove and drain on a wire rack or paper towel.
3 Mix the lettuce, carrot, cucumber and yam slivers in a bowl. Divide between 4 serving bowls and arrange in a pile. Place the fried pumpkin on the top of the pile and make a small indentation in the center. Drop an egg yolk into each indentation and arrange *shiso* leaves around the egg.
4 Serve *ponzu* on the side and pour over salad just before serving.

Seasonal fruit jelly

Shun no furutsu ryo jelli

旬のフルーツ涼ゼリー

Serves 4

1/2 musk melon, halved, seeded, cut
  into five pieces, skinned, and diced,
  substitute with cantaloupe or any ripe
  melon
1 *biwa* (loquat), peeled, seeded, and
  diced, substitute with orange-colored
  fruit such as papaya
8 cherries, pitted without peeling (make
  a small cut to remove the stone)
1/2 *hakuto* (white peach), peeled,
  pitted, and diced
3 litchi (lychee), peeled, pitted, and
  diced
2 cups (500 ml) water
1/2 cup (100 g) sugar
1/6 oz (5 g) gelatin sheets, soaked in
  cold water until softened

The choice of fruit in this dish is entirely up to you but try to use a
variety of appealing colors, so that the fruits trapped in the jelly
look like shimmering jewels.

1 Combine all the diced fruit in a
bowl and mix well.
2 Cut 8 small squares of plastic wrap
and drape over small cups to create
molds. Divide the diced fruit into
four portions and put into the cups
on top of the plastic wrap.
3 Heat the water, sugar, and gelatin
in a saucepan over medium heat
to 194°F (90°C). Stir the mixture
continuously with a wooden
spatula scraping the bottom of the
saucepan to prevent the mixture from
scorching. Remove from heat and
cool by placing the saucepan in a
bowl filled with iced water.
4 When the gelatin begins to
thicken, pour the mixture on top
of the diced fruit, twist the plastic
wrap tightly, then refrigerate.
5 Gently undo and remove the
plastic wrap, then serve wrapped in
bamboo leaves or place the round
jelly directly on a serving dish.

Red bean sherbet

Ogura shabetto

小倉シャーベット

Serves 4
1 3/4 lb (900 g) canned sweet coarse
    azuki bean paste (ogura an), puréed in
    a blender
1 1/4 cups (300 ml) milk
3/4 cup (200 ml) plain syrup

Sweet *azuki* bean paste (*ogura an*) is the basis of all traditional Japanese pastries and desserts. It can be quite sweet and heavy so we have made a lighter version for you to become acquainted with the taste. You can make your own by soaking dried *azuki* beans overnight and slowly simmering the beans with sugar, in the water it was soaked in, to retain the red color and puréeing it to a paste.

1 Heat bean paste, milk, and syrup in a saucepan over medium heat, stirring the mixture continuously with a wooden spatula and scraping the bottom of the saucepan to prevent the mixture from catching. Remove from the heat when it boils.
2 Chill the mixture by pouring it into a bowl set inside a larger bowl filled with iced water. When the mixture is thoroughly cooled, pour into an ice cream machine and follow the manufacturer's instructions.
3 Transfer the bean paste mixture to an airtight container and store in the freezer until ready to serve.

White peach jelly

Hakuto no jelli yose

白桃のゼリー寄せ

Serves 4

6 1/2 oz (200 g) *hakuto* (white peach),
 substitute with yellow peach or
 drained, canned white peach (reserve
 the nectar)
3 tablespoons peach nectar
1/6 oz (5 g) gelatin sheets, soaked
 in cold water until softened
Juice of 1/4 lemon
1/3 cup (75 g) palm sugar, ground with a
 knife, substitute with dark molasses
1/3 cup (65 g) superfine (castor) sugar
Scant 1/2 cup (100 ml) water
5 teaspoons plain syrup
1/2 tablespoon vinegar
4 mint leaves

We have a wide variety of summer delicacies in Japan but the white peach is one of our favorites. This delicious fruit originates from China but, thanks to Marco Polo, the Italians also savor its delicate flavors. In fact, the best place to look for this fruit is in your local Italian deli. Although you can make this dessert with yellow peach or canned white peach, it is well worth looking for white peaches.

1 Peel and grate the peach. It is better not to use a food processor as it breaks down all the fibers and adds too much air. Reserve the grated pulp and the juice.
2 Cut 4 small squares of plastic wrap and drape over small cups to create molds.
3 Place the grated peach pulp, juice, nectar, and gelatin in a saucepan over medium heat. Stir the mixture continuously with a wooden spatula scraping the bottom of the saucepan to prevent it from catching. Remove from heat and add lemon juice when slightly cooled. Cool by placing the saucepan in a bowl filled with iced water until gelatin starts to thicken.

4 Divide the mixture into four portions and pour into the cups on top of the plastic wrap. Twist the plastic wrap tightly around the poured mixture and fix with a rubber band, then cool in iced water until firm.
5 Heat the palm sugar, sugar, water, and syrup in a saucepan over low heat. When the sugar is completely melted, stir in the vinegar, remove from the heat and cool.
6 Pour the molasses in a circle on the serving dish, wipe off the water, unwrap the jelly and place on top of the sauce. Garnish with mint leaves.

Mulberry ice cream

Kuwanomi aiskurimu

桑の実アイスクリーム

Serves 4
2 egg yolks
1/2 in (1 cm) vanilla bean
8 oz (250 g) mulberries
1/3 cup (65 g) sugar
2 cups (500 ml) milk
Scant 1/2 cup (100 ml) heavy (double)
 cream, lightly whipped until thickened
 but not fully whipped
1/8 lemon

Meringue
1/2 egg white
2 teaspoons sugar

1 Whip egg yolks, vanilla bean, and sugar in a bowl with a wire whisk until pale and slightly thickened.
2 Heat the milk in a saucepan over medium heat. Remove from heat just before boiling. Slowly stir the milk into the egg mixture. Return the mixture to the saucepan and heat over medium heat, stirring continuously with a wooden spatula to prevent it from burning. Remove from heat when the mixture starts to thicken.
3 Combine half of the mixture with 6 1/2 oz (200 g) of the mulberries in a blender and purée. Pass through a fine sieve. Pour into a bowl set in a larger bowl filled with iced water. When the mixture is thoroughly cooled, mix with the remaining mixture in an ice cream machine and follow the manufacturer's instructions.
4 To prepare the meringue, whip the egg white with an eggbeater or electric mixer until it is stiff, then beat in the sugar little at a time. Add this and remaining mulberries to the ice cream machine when it is about half frozen.
5 Store in an airtight container in the freezer.

Summer breeze

Kunpu
薫風

Makes 1 cocktail
1 teaspoon *matcha* (powdered green tea), plus extra for decoration
2 fl oz (55 ml) vodka
1 teaspoon squeezed *sudachi* juice, substitute with lemon juice
1/2 teaspoon sugar
1 ice cube

Kunpu is the breeze that wafts in during early summer, carrying with it the aroma of newly opened leaves. The main ingredient of this cocktail—perfect for a summer night—is *matcha*, a powdered green tea used in the tea ceremony. It not only has a beautiful, brilliant green color, but is also rich in vitamin C.

1 Spray a cocktail glass with water. Put some green tea powder (excluding the quantity for the cocktail) into a tea strainer and sprinkle thoroughly on the exterior of the glass.

2 Place all the ingredients into a shaker with a cube of ice, and shake 7 or 8 times. Pour into a glass. Serve immediately and hold the stem of the glass. The surface of the cocktail should be frothy.

autumn

The bountiful colors and aromas of autumn stimulate our appetite. The most representative of the autumn delicacies is the fungus family, and the *matsutake* (pine mushroom) reigns above all the others. The wild fruit to infuse for our therapeutic tonic are also picked during our autumn forest harvests. One cannot expect to find wild fungus along any well-trodden trail or path—a steep incline full of thorny bushes and unbroken cobwebs is a more promising sign of an undiscovered cluster or vine.

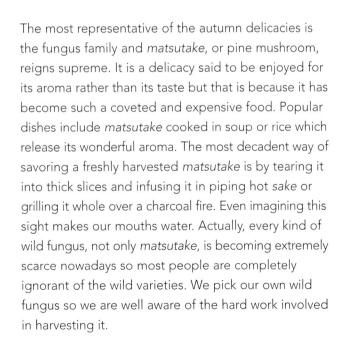

The most representative of the autumn delicacies is the fungus family and *matsutake*, or pine mushroom, reigns supreme. It is a delicacy said to be enjoyed for its aroma rather than its taste but that is because it has become such a coveted and expensive food. Popular dishes include *matsutake* cooked in soup or rice which release its wonderful aroma. The most decadent way of savoring a freshly harvested *matsutake* is by tearing it into thick slices and infusing it in piping hot *sake* or grilling it whole over a charcoal fire. Even imagining this sight makes our mouths water. Actually, every kind of wild fungus, not only *matsutake*, is becoming extremely scarce nowadays so most people are completely ignorant of the wild varieties. We pick our own wild fungus so we are well aware of the hard work involved in harvesting it.

One cannot simply expect to find wild fungus along any trail made by the footsteps of another. A steep incline, full of thorny bushes and unbroken cobwebs, is a promising sign of an undiscovered cluster. It can be a real trek, harvesting the fungus, and even these strenuous expeditions prove to be fruitless at times as the fungus is extremely fickle and susceptible to abnormal climatic conditions, common these days due to global warming. But the joy experienced when we are able to harvest large quantities, especially the extremely rare *chitake*, is extremely worth it. *Chitake*, only known to the fungus connoisseur, is actually even more expensive than the coveted *matsutake* and makes exquisite soup.

above left to right The iron kettle over the fire pit at Yamazaki Farm welcomes us after a strenuous morning of mushroom hunting. The steep incline has left this cluster of *sugi kanako* undiscovered. The autumn *kaki*, or persimmon, display at Yamazaki Farm. A cluster of *modami* fungus. The *tsubadake* safely harvested by the hands of our staff. Autumn Mushroom Salad photographed on site. A harvest of wild fungus: (clockwise from top center) *ura beni hotei shimeji* (*trichloma*), *tsubadake*, *ippon shimeji*, *sugi kanako*, *kuritake* (brick tops), *matsutake* (pine mushroom); (center) *modami* and *houki dake* (broom mushroom).

Wild mushroom hotpot

Kinoko nabe

きのこ鍋

Serves 4
2 2/3 oz (80 g) *chitake* mushrooms
3 1/2 oz (100 g) *shimeji* mushrooms
2 oz (65 g) *hoki dake* mushrooms
2 oz (60 g) *maitake* mushrooms
6 cups (1 1/2 liters) *katsuo dashi* (bonito stock) (see page 248)
1/3 cup (80 ml) *usukuchi shoyu* (light soy sauce)
2 teaspoons natural sea salt
1/4 cup (60 ml) *mirin*

This is one of the treats that we reward ourselves with after a harvest of wild mushrooms. The wild mushrooms can be substituted with any kind of fresh mushroom, such as *shiitake*, portobello, chanterelles, or morels, but it should have a distinctive, woody flavor or a meaty texture. As with all *nabe* (hotpot) dishes, any leftover broth can be made into *zosui* (rice gruel) by adding rice and, in some circumstances, beaten eggs and chopped scallions (spring onions), or *udon* noodles.

1 Trim the stalk ends and any discolored parts from the mushrooms.
2 Wipe the mushrooms with a damp cloth or rinse them quickly in a bowl of water and drain. If you are using morels, or any kind of mushroom which traps dirt, wash thoroughly under running water. If the mushrooms are large, slice into smaller portions.
3 Place the *bonito* stock and all the seasonings in a hot pot and bring to a boil. Lower the heat, add the mushrooms and simmer until the mushrooms are cooked, frequently skimming the foam which floats to the surface.
4 When the mushrooms are cooked, serve in individual bowls, or allow diners to serve themselves directly from the pot.

Autumn mushroom salad

Kinoko no shunju-fu marine

茸の春秋風マリネ

Serves 4
1 oz (30 g) *shimeji* mushrooms
1 oz (30 g) *shiitake* mushrooms
1 oz (30 g) *hita take* mushrooms
1 oz (30 g) *buna hari* mushrooms
1 oz (30 g) *masu take* mushrooms
A few slices lotus root (optional)
2 tablespoons *yuzu ponzu* sauce (see
   page 57), and replace *kabosu* with
   yuzu juice
2 teaspoons vegetable oil

Wild mushrooms are usually blanched and served with grated *daikon*, or pickled in brine to be enjoyed after their short season. However, since we have abundant access to these mushrooms from our harvests, we like to serve them tossed as a salad. The wild mushrooms can be substituted for any kind of fresh, cultivated mushroom, such as *shiitake*, portobello, chanterelles, or morels, but it should have a distinctive woody flavor.

1 Trim the stalk ends from *shimeji* and divide the cluster into individual pieces. Trim the stalk ends from *shiitake* and quarter the cap with the stalk attached. (Trim the stalk ends from *enoki* if using as a replacement for wild mushrooms.) Rinse mushrooms quickly under cold running water and drain.

2 Blanch the mushrooms briefly. Then blanch the lotus root slices, if using.
3 Mix *yuzu ponzu* sauce and vegetable oil with a whisk until well combined, toss with the blanched mushrooms and lotus root slices, and serve.

Quail stuffed with autumn mushrooms

Uzura no kinoko zume
うずらの茸詰め

Serves 4
4 whole quails, cleaned and boned
Few pinches natural sea salt
Pinch black pepper
Vegetable oil for deep-frying ginkgo
    nuts
24 fresh ginkgo nuts, substituted with
    canned or vacuum-packed nuts
4 teaspoons vegetable oil
6 1/2 oz (200 g) *maitake* mushrooms,
    stalk ends removed, cluster split into
    individual peices, substitute with
    shimeji or *shiitake*
6 1/2 tablespoons balsamic vinegar

Many people are reluctant to prepare quail as they are tiny and require a lot of work, but we believe that they are well worth the effort. Quail has delicious meat, especially in the autumn when they are fat and meaty. Be certain that you choose a young bird with firm fat. If the fat feels hard, then the meat will be tough and is unsuitable for broiling.

1 Season the inside of the boned quail with salt and pepper.
2 Heat some vegetable oil in a saucepan over medium-high heat. When the oil is about 176°F (80°C), deep-fry shelled ginkgo nuts to remove their skin. When the skin has split and peeled off in the oil, remove the nut and drain on a wire rack or on paper towels.
3 Heat 4 teaspoons fresh vegetable oil in a saucepan over medium–high heat and sauté the mushrooms, stirring with a wooden spatula so that they do not stick to the bottom of the pan. Season with salt and pepper.
4 When the mushrooms become limp, add the balsamic vinegar and ginkgo nuts and simmer until the liquid is reduced by half.
5 Stuff the quails with the cooled mushroom stuffing and plump them into their original shape.
6 Grill over charcoal or broil under an oven grill until the skin is crispy.

Pine mushroom rice
Matsutake meshi
松茸飯

Serves 4
2 *matsutake* (medium-sized pine mushrooms), about 4 oz (120 g), wiped with
a damp cloth or paper towel, outer
layer of stems shaved off
2 cups + 5 teaspoons (525 ml) *katsuo
dashi* (*bonito* stock) (see page 248)
1 tablespoon *mirin*
1 tablespoon *usukuchi shoyu* (light
soy sauce)
1/2 teaspoon natural seasalt
1 1/2 cups (300 g) Japanese rice (see
page 260 for washing instructions)

The most popular way of cooking *matsutake* fungus (pine mushroom) is to prepare it with rice or in a soup called *dobin mushi,*
made with *hamo* (pike conger) and gingko nuts. Both of these
methods will stretch a few of these precious mushrooms into
substantial dishes. Carefully check for freshness and for telltale
signs of bugs when you purchase this expensive mushroom. As
with the bamboo shoot rice, we like to cook some of our flavored
rice in a Korean stone pot, which will produce a nice crunchy crust,
but a heavy-bottomed enameled pot will do the trick. The recipe is
for the hot rice, which is probably the best way to enjoy the aroma,
but you can also allow it to cool, then make rice patties for an
autumn picnic, as shown in the photograph.

1 Tear mushrooms lengthwise by
hand into 3-mm thick shreds.
2 Heat bonito stock, *mirin*, soy
sauce, and salt in saucepan over
medium heat. Remove from heat
when it begins to boil.
3 Place washed rice, bonito stock
mixture and mushrooms in a heavy-
lidded pot and cook as directed on
page 260. Let stand for 10 minutes,
then heat again over high heat for
4 minutes. This develops a delicious
crunchy crust at the bottom of the pot.
4 Let stand for a further 10 minutes
before fluffing the rice and crust
together with a wooden spatula.
Be careful not to tear the *matsutake*
slices when fluffing the rice.

Hot sake and pine mushroom infusion

Matsutake zake

松茸酒

Serves 4
1/3 oz (10 g) *matsutake* (pine
  mushrooms)
1 1/2 cups (360 ml) *honjozo sake*
  (or other kind of *sake*)

The most luxurious way of appreciating the splendid aroma and texture of the precious *matsutake* is to grill it whole or sliced in half over charcoal. The piping hot *matsutake* oozing with its juices should be torn lengthwise with fingers and quickly dipped into the highest quality soy sauce spiked with *sudachi*, a small green citrus which is an absolute accompaniment for *matsutake*. Another wonderful method is to use some slices in piping hot *sake*. Carefully check for freshness and for telltale signs of bugs when you purchase this expensive mushroom.

1 Pine mushroom should never be washed or dipped in water as you will lose some of its wonderful aroma. It should always be carefully wiped with a damp cloth or paper towel. The stalk ends should not be sliced off, but shaved off using a knife since the stalk is very thick, the inside of the stalk end can be eaten.

2 Heat *sake* and mushroom slices in a saucepan over medium heat. Remove from heat just before boiling. Serve in a *dobin*, or ceramic teapot, which can be found in Japanese grocery stores, or in a small iron teakettle with *sake* cups.

Wild fruit and herb-infused tonics

Kajitsu shu

果実酒

These tonics are made by macerating fruit or herbs in plain *shochu*, a vodka-like distilled spirit (made from rice, barley, potato or sugar cane) and rock sugar. Although most tonics can be consumed after just three months, the flavors mellow significantly with age and some tonics, such as *umeshu* (Japanese apricot wine), can be aged indefinitely. Choose your favorite fruits or herbs and, if you can't find *shochu* in Japanese stores (sold as *soju* in Korean stores), use vodka instead. If using soft, ripe fruit such as berries, it is best to remove them after they impart their flavor and color, and before they begin to disintegrate. The tonics are served on the rocks or with a splash of soda or water.

Pear tonic (*ra furansu shu*)

(for constipation, digestive disorders, and the common cold)

2 lb (900 g) Western pears (e.g. La France, Bartlett), washed

14 oz (450 g) lemons, peeled and thickly sliced

7 oz (225 g) rock sugar

1 3/4 quarts (1 3/4 liters) rum

1 Place pear, lemon, and sugar into a wide-mouthed bottle or preserve jar, add *shochu* and store for a minimum of 3 months in a cool, dark place. Stir occasionally to melt the sugar.

2 Remove the fruit after 3 months, pour through a fine sieve and store.

Japanese apricot tonic (*ume shu*)

(for fatigue, loss of appetite, insomnia, diarrhea, back pain, cold prevention, respiratory disorders, and arthritis)

2 lb (1 kg) *ume* (Japanese apricots), soaked overnight (available early summer)

1 3/4 quarts (1 3/4 liters) *shochu*

1 lb (500 g) rock sugar

1 Wash the apricots, rubbing the skin, taking care not to bruise the fruit. Place fruit and sugar alternately into a wide-mouthed bottle or preserve jar, add *shochu* and store for a minimum of 3 months in a cool, dark place. Stir occasionally to melt the sugar.

Cinnamon tonic (*nikki shu*)

(for fatigue, headaches, loss of appetite, stomach pain, blood circulation, and digestive disorders)

3 oz (90 g) cinnamon bark or sticks, stems and dried leaves discarded

1 3/4 quarts (1 3/4 liters) *shochu*

1/2 cup (125 g) sugar

Place cinnamon and sugar into a wide-mouthed bottle or preserve jar, add *shochu* and store for 2 months in a cool, dark place.

2 Remove the cinnamon after 2 months, pour through a fine sieve and store again for a minimum of 6 months.

Gomishi tonic

(for fatigue, coughing, respiratory disorders, asthma, and depression)

8 oz (250 g) *gomishi* (a wild berry indigenous to Japan and Korea), stems and dried leaves discarded, washed

1 3/4 quarts (1 3/4 liters) *shochu*

1/2 cup (125 g) sugar

1 Place fruit and sugar into a wide mouthed bottle or preserve jar, add *shochu* and store for a minimum of 3 months in a cool, dark place.

2 Remove the fruit after 3months, pour through a fine sieve and store. If using dried berries, they can be left in the jar.

Catnip tonic (*matatabi shu*)

(see opposite)

(for fatigue, constipation, anemia, and urinary disorders)

8 oz (250 g) catnip fruit, washed

1 3/4 quarts (1 3/4 liters) *shochu*

1/2 cup (125 g) sugar

1 Place catnip and sugar into a wide-mouthed bottle or preserve jar, add *shochu* and store for a minimum of 3 months in a cool, dark place.

2 Remove the fruit after 3 months, pour through a fine sieve and store.

Strawberry tonic (*ichigo shu*)

(see below right)
(for skin disorders, fatigue, and the
common cold)
2 lb (1 kg) strawberries (available in
early April)
6 1/2 oz (200 g) lemons
1 3/4 quarts (1 3/4 liters) *shochu*
Scant 1 cup (200 g) sugar

1 Wash the strawberries, taking care
not to bruise the fruit. Peel the
lemons thickly to remove the peel
and pith, and slice crosswise into
1/2-in (1-cm) thick slices.
2 Pour *shochu* into a wide-mouthed
bottle or preserve jar, add the strawberries, remove the stems, and add
the lemon and sugar. Store for 2
months in a cool, dark place.
3 Remove the fruit after 2 months,
pour through a fine sieve and store.

Bayberry tonic (*yamamomo shu*)

(for fatigue, loss of appetite, digestive
disorders, and diarrhea)
6 1/2 oz (200 g) ripe bayberries, washed
(available early summer)
1 3/4 quarts (1 3/4 liters) *shochu*
1/2 cup (125 g) sugar

1 Wash the bayberries, taking
care not to bruise the fruit. Place
bayberries and sugar into a wide-
mouthed bottle or preserve jar, add
shochu and store for a minimum
of 3 months in a cool, dark place.
2 Remove the fruit after 3 months,
pour through a fine sieve and store.

Raspberry tonic (*ki ichigo shu*)

(for fatigue, loss of appetite, blood
circulation, insomnia, and digestion)
2 lb (1 kg) raspberries (available in
mid May)
1 3/4 quarts (1 3/4 liters) *shochu*
10 1/2 oz (315 g) rock sugar
14 oz (450 g) lemons

1 Wash the raspberries, taking care
not to bruise the fruit. Peel the
lemons thickly to remove the peel
and pith, and slice crosswise into
1/2-in (1-cm) thick slices.
2 Place sugar, raspberries, and lemon
into a wide-mouthed bottle or preserve jar, add *shochu* and store for 2
months in a cool, dark place.
3 Remove the fruit after 2 months,
pour through a fine sieve and store.

Hasukappu tonic

(for fatigue, insomnia, anemia, and
digestive disorders)
2 lb (1 kg) *hasukappu* (a wild berry
indigenous to Hokkaido, available
in late May)
1 3/4 quarts (1 3/4 liters) *shochu*
3 1/2 oz (100 g) rock sugar
3 1/2 oz (100 g) lemons

1 Wash the berries, taking care not
to bruise the fruit. Peel the lemons
thickly to remove the peel and pith,
and slice crosswise into 1/2-in (1-cm)
thick slices.
2 Place sugar, berries, and lemon into
a wide-mouthed bottle or preserve
jar, add *shochu* and store for at least
3 months in a cool, dark place. Stir
occasionally to melt the sugar.

Pine needle tonic (*matsuba shu*)

(see below right)

(for high blood pressure, heart ailments, and arthritis)

6 1/2 oz (200 g) young pine needles (available in early January)
1 3/4 quarts (1 3/4 liters) *shochu*
1/4 cup (75 g) sugar

1 Wash the pine needles thoroughly, dry and cut into 1 in (2 1/2 cm) lengths.
2 Place needles in a bottle, add *shochu* and store for at least 3 months in a cool, dark place. (The pine needles carbonate so only loosely cover the mouth of the bottle, such as with paper and string, as the bottle may explode.)
3 Remove the pine needles after 3 months, pour through a fine sieve and store. Can be also drunk as a very strong cider when it starts to carbonate.

Mullberry tonic (*kuwa no mi*)

(for fatigue, constipation, urinary disorders, and anemia)

8 oz (250 g) lemons
2 1/2 oz (75 g) rock sugar
1 lb (500 g) ripe mulberries, washed (available early summer)
1 3/4 quarts (1 3/4 liters) *shochu*

1 Wash the mulberries, taking care not to bruise the fruit. Peel the lemons thickly to remove the peel and pith, and slice crosswise into 1/2-in (1-cm) thick slices.
2 Place sugar, mulberries, and lemon into a wide-mouthed bottle or preserve jar, add *shochu* and store for 2 months in a cool, dark place.
3 Remove the fruit after 2 months, pour through a fine sieve and store.

Apricot tonic (*anzu shu*)

(for fatigue, loss of appetite, coughing, asthma, swelling, and cold prevention).

2 lb (1 kg) apricots (available early summer), carefully washed
1 3/4 quarts (1 3/4 liters) *shochu*
Scant 1 cup (200 g) sugar

1 Wash the apricots, rubbing the skin, taking care not to bruise the fruit. Remove the stems using a bamboo skewer or toothpick. Place fruit and sugar alternately into a wide-mouthed bottle or preserve jar, add *shochu* and store for a minimum of 3 months in a cool, dark place. Stir occasionally to melt the sugar.
2 Remove the fruit after 3 months, pour through a fine sieve and store.

Autumn starters

Aki no otoshi
秋のお通し

Serves 4

Puréed chestnut balls (*kuri no chakin*)
10 chestnuts braised in syrup, drained
1 egg yolk
1 teaspoon black sesame seeds

1 Preheat oven to 356°F (180°C).
2 Purée the chestnuts in a food processor to form a smooth paste. Add the egg yolk and blend again.
3 Divide the mixture into 2/3-oz (20-g) portions and place on individual pieces of plastic wrap. Twist the plastic wrap tightly around the mixture and form into a ball with a twisted top.
4 Carefully remove the plastic wrap, place on a cookie sheet, and bake for 5 minutes. Remove from the oven and sprinkle with sesame seeds. Serve hot or at room temperature.

Smoked duck (*aigamo no sumoku*)
1 duck breast, about 6 1/2 oz (200 g)
15 tablespoons (30 g) *Herbes de Provence*
2 teaspoons freshly ground black pepper
4 teaspoons natural sea salt
2 1/2 teaspoons sugar
1/2 cup (120 ml) water
6 1/2 oz (200 g) mixed *sakura* (cherry tree) and apple tree chips

1 Prick duck breast skin so that it will absorb the seasonings well.
2 Mix all the ingredients except tree chips, and marinate the duck for about 3 hours. Wipe the moisture off the duck, wrap in plastic wrap, and refrigerate for 2 days.
3 Smoke the duck in a home smoker (or covered wok) for 10 minutes with the wood chips. Cool and slice diagonally into thin slices.

Halibut sashimi (*hirame no negi maki*)
1/3 oz (10 g) *fugu negi* (welsh or ciboule onion), substitute with green stalks of thin scallions (spring onions)
1 1/3 oz (40 g) sashimi-quality halibut fillet

1 Cut the *fugu negi* into 2-in (5-cm) lengths, and the halibut using *sogi giri* cut (see page 247)
3 Roll each piece of halibut sashimi with a few pieces of scallion. Serve immediately or place in a container covered with plastic wrap until ready to serve. Consume within 2 hours.

Sardine tartar minced with miso (*iwashi no miso tataki*)
2 sashimi-quality sardines, 3 1/2 oz (100 g)
1/3 oz (10 g) *fugu negi* (welsh or ciboule onion), substitute with green stalks of thin scallions (spring onions)
2 1/2 tablespoons *naga negi* (long welsh onion), substitute with white part of scallion (spring onion)
1/2-in (1.2-cm) ginger
1 tablespoon *aka* miso (red miso), to garnish
1 teaspoon white sesame seeds

1 Prepare the sardines into a three-section fillet (see page 244).
2 Cut the *fugu negi* crosswise finely; mince the *naga negi* finely; and peel and grate the ginger. Then mince the filleted sardines on the chopping board finely with a sharp knife.
3 Place the minced sardines in a bowl and mix with all the ingredients. This can be prepared ahead of time and reserved in the refrigerator. When serving, place a circular mold with an open top such a cookie cutter in the middle of the serving platter and press the minced sardine mixture into the mold. Sprinkle a little chopped *fugu negi* and sesame seeds on top, and remove the mold. Serve immediately.

Salt-broiled ginkgo nuts (*shio ginnan*)
20 ginkgo nuts in the shell
2 tablespoons natural sea salt

1 Slightly crack the nuts but do not open. Soak for a few minutes.
2 Place salt in a skillet over medium heat, shaking the pan so that the salt does not scorch. When the salt heats through, place the nuts in the pan and heat for several minutes, shaking the pan constantly. When the ginkgo nuts are thoroughly cooked (they become apple green), remove from pan and serve with the salt. Crack them open with your fingers to eat.

Shrimp-stuffed *shiitake* (*shiitake ebi surimi zume*)
4 *shiitake* mushrooms
2 2/3 oz (80 g) puréed white flesh fish
4 oz (120 g) black tiger prawns
1/4 onion
4 teaspoons mayonnaise
Pinch natural sea salt
Pinch white pepper
1 tablespoon all-purpose (plain) flour
Vegetable oil

1 Trim the stalk ends from *shiitake*.
2 Shell and devein the shrimp and blend to a smooth paste. Blend the fish fillets to a smooth paste.
3 Mince the onions finely and sauté in some oil until soft. Set aside in a bowl. Combine shrimp, fish, onions, mayo, salt and pepper.
4 Dust the inner sides of the caps of *shiitake* mushrooms with flour and stuff with the shrimp/fish stuffing. Lightly dust with flour and deep-fry in 356°F (180°C) oil until lightly browned, about 2 minutes. Drain on paper towels and serve immediately.

Grilled smoked autumn salmon belly

Aki jake harasumi kunsei yaki

秋鮭はらす身薫製焼き

Serves 4
6 1/2–8 oz (200–250 g) salmon *harasumi* (belly)
Natural sea salt
4 *sakura* (Japanese cherry wood) logs, about 12 x 4 in (30 x 10 cm), substitute with cherry wood chips
5 *sumi* (wood charcoal) logs, about 4 in (10 cm) long, replace with charcoal briquettes
1 *sudachi*, halved, substitute with lemon wedges

Shirozake (chum or dog salmon) from the northern waters of Japan is considered at its best in October when it returns to the streams where it was born for spawning. Traditionally, the only way to serve salmon was to preserve the fish in salt and grill it. Salmon sushi, popular outside of Japan where varieties of fish are limited, probably developed from the regional Hokkaido dish called *ruibe* which is thinly sliced, frozen, raw salmon. The belly of the autumn salmon is fatty and well suited for smoking.

1 Cut the salmon belly lengthwise into 3 or 4 strips (depending on the size of the salmon), each strip about 4 cm (1 1/2 in) wide.
2 Parch the sea salt in a skillet over low heat taking care not to burn the salt. There should be enough salt to cover the salmon lightly. Salt the salmon strips.
3 Light the charcoal on a grill or in a charcoal chimney starter until red-hot and place inside a smoker. Light the cherry wood log on a grill, let it burn until it begins to smoke, then blow out the flame and transfer it to the smoker. Alternatively, scatter cherry wood chips over the charcoal.
4 When the smoker is filled with smoke, place the salmon belly strips on the grill inside the smoker. Cover, and smoke for 7 to 8 minutes. Carefully turn the salmon over and smoke for another 7 to 8 minutes. The fish should be quite rare inside. Set aside.
5 Just before serving, charcoal grill the salmon over high heat so that it is slightly browned and a bit crispy to touch. Serve with halved *sudachi* or lemon wedges.

Seared autumn bonito sashimi with apple mustard dressing

Modori gatsuo no yofu jitate

戻りかつおのたたき洋風仕立て

Serves 4

400 g (13 oz) *katsuo* (bonito) fillet with skin, cut in three-section fillet (see page 244), try to buy a filleted piece as even a small fish is quite large

Dressing

1/4 cup (50 g) onion, grated
1/3 cup (40 g) apple, grated
1/3 cup (100 ml) *su* (rice vinegar)
1/4 cup (60 ml) *sake*
1/2 cup (120 ml) *koikuchi shoyu* (soy sauce)
2 teaspoons sesame oil
4 teaspoons vegetable oil
2 teaspoons coarse-grain mustard
1/2 teaspoon superfine (castor) sugar
1/2 teaspoon *shichimi togarashi* (seven spice chili powder)
1 teaspoon white sesame seeds
4 medium cloves (10 g) garlic, grated
1 in (2.5 cm) ginger
1/3 oz (10 g) *naga negi* (long welsh onion), substitute with white part of scallion (spring onion), finely minced

Garnish

1 oz (30 g) *daikon*, cut in thin slivers and refreshed in cold water (see page 251)
1 oz (30 g) *kyuri* (Japanese cucumber), substitute with deseeded Western cucumber, cut in thin slivers and refreshed in cold water (see page 251),
1 teaspoon *murame,* omit if unavailable
2 1/2 tablespoons *banno negi*, substitute with fine scallions (sping onions), finely chopped crossways
5 *shiso* (perilla) leaves, cut in thin slivers

Traveling on the Kuroshio current, *katsuo* (skipjack or bonito) arrives in Japanese waters in the spring and autumn of each year. The autumn bonito that is caught off the northern shores of Japan is especially delicious. Growing up to 3 meters in length and 700 kilograms in weight, this large fish is extremely important in Japanese cuisine as it is the source of *kezuribushi*, dried fillet shavings, which are used to produce *katsuo dashi* or bonito stock. Bonito sashimi is always served as *tataki*—the fillet is seared leaving the inside raw—and the ruby colored flesh contrasts beautifully with the charred black skin.

1 Place the fillet skin-side-down on a cutting board and pierce the side with three metal skewers in a fan shape. Sprinkle the flesh lightly with sea salt. Hold the skewered fillet, skin-side-down, over a high gas flame. When the oil begins to bubble and drip and the skin is nicely charred, turn around and sear the other side lightly. Plunge into iced water for 15 seconds to arrest the cooking process.
2 Pat excess moisture away and slice into brick cut (see page 245) about 1/2 in (1 cm) thick. Arrange on a platter, the sliced side facing up, in a circular pattern.
3 Combine all the dressing ingredients and mix thoroughly with a whisk. Pour the dressing on and around the fish slices.
4 To arrange the garnish, pile the daikon and cucumber slivers in the middle of the fish slices and top with *akame*, chopped *banno negi*, and *shiso* leaf slivers.

Whisk-cut braised eggplants

Ni nasu

煮茄子

Serves 4

5 cups (1 1/4 liters) *katsuo dashi* (bonito stock) (see page 248)

3/4 cup (200 ml) *koikuchi shoyu* (soy sauce)

3/4 cup (200 ml) *mirin*

8 *nasu* (Japanese eggplants), substitute with small eggplants, cut in whisk cut (see page 251)

3/4 cup (200 ml) chilled *katsuo dashi* (bonito stock) (see page 248)

Garnish

Naga negi (long welsh onion), substitute with white part of scallion (spring onion), cut in thin slivers and refreshed in cold water (see page 251)

Ginger, peeled, cut in thin slivers and refreshed in cold water (see page 251)

Chasen giri, or whisk cutting, is one of the first knife skills learned by Japanese chefs. Chefs in traditional Japanese kitchens follow a very strict apprenticeship system. An apprentice chef is not even allowed to touch a knife until he has completed a few years of scrubbing the kitchen floor and polishing the utensils. If a dedicated learner has survived this grueling apprenticeship, he is often presented with one vegetable knife by the master chef and whisk cutting is one of the many techniques that he must practice for months before receiving a stamp of approval by his master.

1 Heat the 5 cups bonito stock (not the chilled stock), soy, and *mirin* in a saucepan over medium heat until boiling. Lower the heat, add eggplants and simmer for 20 minutes. 2 To brighten the color of the eggplants dulled by the simmering, add the chilled bonito stock to the saucepan and simmer for a further 20 minutes.

3 Remove the eggplants with a slotted spoon, lightly twist them and place in a serving bowl. Spoon over some of the cooking liquid, then garnish with the slivers of ginger and *naga negi*. Serve warm.

Grilled soybean lees dumplings

Okara dango

おから団子

Serves 4
1 egg yolk
Scant 1/3 cup (80 ml) heavy (double) cream
2 teaspoons Korean virgin sesame oil
2 teaspoons vegetable oil
1 lb 5 oz (600 g) *okara* (tofu lees), excess liquid sqeezed off (see page 254)
1 teaspoon natural sea salt
Pinch white pepper

Sauce
Scant 1 1/2 cups (360 ml) *katsuo dashi* (bonito stock) (see page 248)
4 teaspoons *mirin*
1 teaspoon *yuzu togarashi* (seven spice chili powder mixed with dried *yuzu*, or Japanese citron), substitute by adding grated lemon peel to seven spice chili powder
3 tablespoons (12 g) *kuzu* (*kudzu* starch), substitute with cornstarch, dissolved in 2 1/2 teaspoons water
12 *menegi* (welsh onion sprouts), substitute with chives

Try this recipe when you prepare soymilk for the tofu recipes since tofu lees, a by-product of the soymilk recipe is required here. It is actually the bran residue of soybean when you filter soymilk. Tofu lees, known as *okara* in Japanese, is very rich in protein and is an essential component of a Buddhist monk's cuisine. However, since it is quite bland and dry, we have added a variety of ingredients to make it moist and tasty.

1 Beat the egg yolk with the heavy cream. Set aside.
2 Heat the sesame and vegetable oils in a saucepan over high heat and add the tofu lees. Stir continuously with a wooden spatula to prevent it catching the bottom of the pan, until all the moisture has evaporated. When the tofu lees is dry and crumbly, remove from heat and empty into a bowl. Season with salt and pepper, and add the egg yolk mixture a little at a time, mixing well with a spatula.
3 Divide the mixture into eight pieces, wrap each piece with plastic wrap and roll into a ball. Steam the wrapped balls for 10 minutes. Let cool and refrigerate overnight.
4 Heat some vegetable oil in a heavy skillet and fry the refrigerated dumplings over medium high heat until nicely browned.
5 To prepare the sauce, heat the stock, *mirin*, and *yuzu togarashi* in saucepan over medium heat. Stir in the dissolved starch and remove from heat when the sauce is thickened. Pour the sauce over the grilled dumplings and garnish with *menegi*.

Tofu topped with scallion and baby anchovies
Jako negi dofu
じゃこ葱豆腐

Serves 4

2 blocks tofu, about 1 lb 5 oz (600 g), excess water drained off (to make homemade block tofu from freshly curdled tofu (see page 108), pack the drained soft tofu firmly in a container, smooth the surface and refrigerate until firm, then to unmold, cover the container with a flat dish or cutting board and flip the container upside down slowly)

3 oz (80 g) *banno negi*, substitute with with scallions (spring onions), finely chopped

4 teaspoons vegetable oil

8 teaspoons sesame oil

4 oz (120 g) *takana* (pickled mustard greens), finely chopped, optional but if omitted add a pinch of salt

4 oz (120 g) *jako* (baby air-cured anchovies), available in Japanese grocery stores

1/2 tablespoon *koikuchi shoyu* (soy sauce)

1 teaspoon *sake*

Our other tofu recipes feature the fluffy freshly made version, which is not available in stores outside of Japan, as far as we know. This recipe, however, uses the firmer block tofu which is made from homemade tofu, or can be substituted by the store-bought version. We prefer *momen*, the firmer kind, but if you like the softer kind, it can be used here as well.

1 Cut each block of tofu into two and arrange the four blocks on a dish. Pile the finely chopped *banno negi* on top.

2 Heat the vegetable oil and half of the sesame oil over medium heat in a heavy skillet. Add chopped *takana* (if using) and fry lightly. When the oil becomes hot, add *jako* and stir continuously. When the oil begins to foam, remove *takana* and *jako* with a slotted spoon and place on top of the chopped *banno negi*.

3 Add the remaining sesame oil to the pot and heat. Remove from heat. Add soy sauce and *sake*, and mix well. Pour over the tofu and serve immediately.

Charcoal-broiled lamb chops

Kohitsuji niku no sumibi yaki

仔羊肉の炭火焼き

Serves 4
1 tablespoon vegetable oil
2 cloves garlic, finely chopped
5 oz (150 g) onion, finely chopped
2/3 cup (180 ml) red wine
Scant 1 1/2 cups (360 ml) chili sauce
1/4 cup (60 ml) Worcester sauce
Scant 1/4 cup (50 g) sugar
Pinch natural sea salt
Pinch black pepper
Pinch *Herbes de Provence*
4 lamb chops, about 4 oz (120 g) each

With the introduction of French and Italian cuisine over the past years, many Japanese have begun to enjoy lamb and we often include it in our grilled menus. Since we really don't offer a main course at Shunju—our clients like to share their dishes—this recipe is more suited to serving along with other dishes; it is also heavily spiced.

1 Heat the oil in a saucepan over medium heat and sauté the garlic until lightly browned. Add the chopped onion and sauté until translucent.

2 Add the red wine, flambé and burn off the alcohol content. When the flame has subsided, add the chili sauce, Worcester sauce, sugar, salt, pepper, and *Herbes de Provence*. Simmer for 10 minutes.

3 Remove from heat, pour into a shallow container large enough to accommodate the lamb chops in a single layer and let cool.

4 When the marinade has cooled, add the lamb chops and marinate for 2 hours.

5 Wipe off the excess marinade from the lamb chops, grill over charcoal and serve immediately.

Roasted North Sea duck and apple

Hokkai gamo to ringo no rosuto

北海鴨とりんごのロースト

Serves 4
5 red apples, washed
8 cups (2 liters) water with
  2 tablespoons salt added
3/4 cup (180 ml) *katsuo dashi*
  (bonito stock) (see page 248)
Pinch natural sea salt
2 1/2 teaspoons butter
Pinch white pepper
1 tablespoon *usukuchi shoyu* (light
  soy sauce)
Pinch natural sea salt
2 tablespoons vegetable oil
6 oz (200 g) Hokkai (or other) duck
  breast, fat trimmed off, scored on one
  side in a crisscross pattern, seasoned
  with salt and pepper
3 teaspoons (15 g) butter

We use duck in many of our recipes in our restaurants. This is a simple roasted duck recipe presented beautifully in an apple casing. All our meat dishes are sliced into bite-sized pieces so that they can be eaten with chopsticks.

1 Preheat oven to 356°F (180°C, gas 4).

2 Slice the top off four of the apples (slice crosswise about 1/4 way down the apple). Hollow out the four apples to about half of their depth using a spoon or a melon baller. Reserve the pulp. Soak the hollowed apple casings and the tops in the salted water to prevent oxidation and discoloring. Set aside.

3 To make apple sauce, remove the core and seeds from the reserved apple pulp and add to a saucepan with bonito stock and a pinch of sea salt. Simmer for about 10 minutes or until soft. Transfer to a blender and purée. Then push through a sieve to yield a smooth purée. Combine the apple purée in a saucepan with butter, pepper, soy sauce, and salt and heat over medium heat. When thoroughly combined, remove from heat and set aside.

4 Trim off fat from the duck breast. Make a crisscross pattern on one side by making shallow diagonal incisions. Season with salt and pepper.

5 Heat the vegetable oil in a oven-proof skillet or pan over medium heat. Place the duck, crisscross pattern side down, in the pan and sauté until nicely browned. Flip and sauté the other side lightly. Place the pan into the oven and roast for about 5 or 6 minutes until medium rare (or longer as desired). Remove from oven and set aside.

6 Meanwhile, peel the remaining apple, slice it in half lengthwise, then halve again. Remove the core and seeds and slice the wedges into 5-mm-thick slices. Season with salt and pepper. Heat the butter in a skillet over low heat, add the apple slices and sauté until lightly browned. Remove from pan.

7 Slice the duck into 16 slices. Remove the apple casings from the water and pat dry. Pour some apple sauce into the casing, add a slice of sautéed apple, then a slice of duck. Continue to layer until apple is full. Repeat for all four apple casings. Cover with the apple tops.

Duck and scallion miso grilled on magnolia leaf

Kamo negi miso no hoba yaki

鴨葱味噌の朴葉焼き

Serves 4

10 oz (400 g) duck breast, cut in 1/2-in (1-cm) cubes
3 1/2 oz (100 g) *naga negi* (long welsh onion), substitute with white part of scallion (spring onion), thinly sliced
1/2 cup (120 ml) *sake*
1/4 cup (60 ml) *mirin*
10 oz (400 g) *koji* miso
1/2 cup (100 g) superfine (castor) sugar
2 oz (50 g) *banno negi*, substitute with green tops of scallions (spring onions), finely chopped
4 dried magnolia leaves, soaked then patted dry

Hoba yaki, translated as grilled on a magnolia leaf, is a favorite treat for *sake* lovers. To lick the salty miso and enjoy a leisurely sip of *sake,* is undeniably "*iki*" (enlightenment). If you are able to find a beautiful charcoal brazier made in ceramic, iron or stone in a Japanese/Asian antique or houseware store, it makes a dramatic presentation on a chilly autumn evening. It is well worth the investment as you can grill air-cured fish, vegetables, and meat (although it can get quite smoky) or even place a hotpot on the brazier. Not only does it make a beautiful visual presentation but it also allows you to cook at the table.

1 Sauté the duck in a saucepan over medium heat. As the duck meat releases a lot of oil, remove the duck from the pan with a slotted spoon and discard the oil. Return duck to the pan, together with chopped *naga negi*, and add *sake* and *mirin* when *naga negi* becomes limp. Boil off the alcohol.
2 Reduce the heat to low and add miso and sugar and cook for about ten minutes until a smooth paste is formed, stirring constantly with a wooden ladle to prevent scorching.
3 Spread duck and miso paste on the leaf, garnish with *banno negi*. Place the leaf on a charcoal brazier at the table and grill until miso starts to bubble.

Grilled beef ribs marinated in rice wine

Hone tsuki karubi no shokoshu zuke yaki

骨付カルビの紹興酒漬け焼き

Serves 4

1 cup (240 ml) *mirin*

1 3/4 lb (800 g) beef short ribs, have your butcher slice the ribs crosswise into 1/2-in (1-cm) thick slices with the bone attached on each edge, otherwise slice pre-cut ribs lengthwise leaving the last piece with the bone, substitute with thinly sliced sirloin or T-bone

1 1/4 cups (300 ml) *shaoxing* Chinese rice wine, substitute with dry sherry

1/4 cups (300 ml) *katsuo dashi* (bonito stock) (see page 248)

1 cup (240 ml) *koikuchi shoyu* (soy sauce)

1 in (2.5 cm) ginger, sliced

5 oz (150 g) *naga negi* (long welsh onion), substitute with white part of scallion (spring onion)

10 oz (300 g) arugula

Shaoxing is a kind of rice wine fermented from medium-grain sticky (*mochi*) rice in the Shaoxing province of China. We serve it warmed on chilly evenings and chilled on the rocks in the warmer months. It is also an important seasoning in the Chinese kitchen, used for flavoring and, most dramatically, as a marinade in which live prawns are infused at the table.

1 Remove the alcohol content from the *mirin*, by bringing it to a boil in a small saucepan.

2 Combine all the ingredients except for the arugula in a container large enough to fit the meat.

Marinate overnight in the refrigerator.

3 Wipe the excess marinade from the meat and grill it over charcoal or on a stovetop grill.

4 Serve on a bed of arugula.

Grilled lotus root patties

Renkon mochi no isobe yaki

蓮根もちの磯辺焼き

1/3 cup (85 ml) *katsuo dashi* (bonito stock) (see page 248)
3 1/2 teapsoons *mirin*
3 1/2 teapsoons *koikuchi shoyu* (soy sauce)
1 lb (500 g) *renkon* (lotus root) washed and peeled, cut into wedges (slice diagonally, turn lotus a quarter turn then slice again, repeat)
4 teaspoons *su* (rice vinegar)
3 oz (90 g) *katakuri* starch, substitute with potato starch
1 1/3 oz (40 g) *joshinko* (non-glutinous rice flour)
Pinch sea salt
Pinch white pepper
2 tablespoons vegetable oil
1 sheet *nori*, cut into 8 pieces

Vegetable patties frequently appear on our menus using seasonal vegetables such as *nasu* (eggplant), and *shungiku* (chrysanthemum leaves). *Isobe yaki* means grilled with soy sauce and wrapped with *nori* (laver) and the grilled rice *mochi* is a popular snack and street vendor food.

1 Preheat oven to 356°F (180°C, gas 4).
2 Mix bonito stock, *mirin*, and soy sauce and reserve.
3 Place lotus root wedges in a saucepan with enough water to cover, add rice vinegar and heat over medium heat for 30 minutes. Drain in a colander and purée in a food processor. Transfer to a bowl and mix with *katakuri* starch and rice flour, and season with salt and white pepper.
4 Mold this mixture into flat patties, approximately 2 oz (70 g) each. Fry the patties in an oven-ready skillet or pan coated with the vegetable oil.
5 When one side is lightly browned, flip, remove pan from heat and place it in the oven. Bake for 6 or 7 minutes. Remove from the oven and add the reserved soy sauce mixture and heat over low heat until the sauce thickens.
6 When the patties are coated and the sauce thickened, remove from heat and wrap each patty with a slice of *nori*.

Steamed Japanese yam and duck dumplings

Yama imo manju

山芋饅頭

Serves 4
2 lb (900 g) *yama imo* (Japanese yam),
  substitute with Chinese yam (but not
  Western potato), peeled and cut in
  1/2-in (1-cm) slices
2 egg whites
Pinch natural sea salt
Vegetable oil
4 oz (120 g) coarsley ground duck breast
3 1/2 oz (100 g) *maitake* (hen-of-the-
  woods fungus), substitute with any
  kind of meaty fungus, stems/roots
  discarded
12 ginkgo nuts, shelled and boiled with
  a pinch of salt, thick skin removed
  (see Note)
3 1/2 tablespoons *koikuchi shoyu* (soy
  sauce)
3 1/2 tablespoons *mirin*
1 1/4 cups (300 ml) *katsuo dashi* (bonito
  stock) (see page 248)
Pinch finely chopped *yuzu* (Japanese
  citron) peel
1 teaspoon *katakuri* starch, substitute
  with potato starch dissolved in
  1 teaspoon water
1 teaspoon *usukuchi shoyu* (light soy
  sauce)
Pinch natural sea salt

In Japan, yam is an autumn specialty. The most common way to eat it is to grate and mix it with bonito stock, seasoned with soy sauce. This mixture is then poured over hot steamed rice and barley, or used as a dipping sauce for cold *soba* buckwheat noodles. Or the yams can be sliced into thin julienne strips and served sashimi-style with soy sauce and wasabi. As raw yam has a very slippery texture and can cause an allergic reaction in some, we use it steamed.

1 Steam *yama imo* slices for 10 minutes over high heat. Mash over a sieve. Transfer to a bowl, add egg whites and a pinch of sea salt, and mix thoroughly.
2 Heat vegetable oil in a saucepan over medium heat and sauté the ground duck. When the duck is lightly browned, add fungus and ginkgo nuts.
3 Stir in soy sauce, *mirin*, 1/2 cup (100 ml) of the bonito stock, and *yuzu* peel. Bring to a boil, remove from heat, and add half of the dissolved starch mixture. Set this filling mixture aside.
4 Divide the mashed *yama imo* into four portions and make four patties. Spoon one quarter of the filling into the center of the patty and roll into a ball. Place the ball into a piece of cheesecloth and twist the top. Remove from cloth. Steam the dumplings for about 5 minutes.
5 Bring remaining bonito stock, light soy sauce, and pinch of salt to a boil in a saucepan over medium heat. Add remaining starch mixture and remove from heat when sauce is slightly thickened.
6 Spoon the sauce over the steamed dumplings.

Note: An easier way to remove ginkgo skins is to cover them with boiling water and 1/3 teaspoon baking soda and stir vigorously. Drain and rinse well.

Griddle cakes

Maru yaki
丸焼き

Serves 4
For one griddle cake
2 2/3 oz (80 g) French bread dough
2 tablespoons sesame oil
All-purpose (plain) flour

Prawn and garlic chive filling
2 teaspoons vegetable oil
1 1/3 oz (40 g) black tiger prawns,
  shelled and deveined, cut in 1/2-in
  (1-cm) pieces, lightly pounded with the
  blunt edge of a knife
1/2 teaspoon natural sea salt
Pinch white pepper
1 handful garlic chives, washed and cut
  in 2-in (5-cm) lengths
2 tablespoons katsuo dashi (bonito
  stock) (see page 248)
4 teaspoons tomato catsup (ketchup)
3 tablespoons katakuri starch, substitute
  with potato starch dissolved in
  4 teaspoons water

Duck and walnut miso filling
2 teaspoons vegetable oil
1 1/3 oz (40 g) duck breast, cut in 1/2-in
  (1-cm) cubes
4 teaspoons mirin
2/3 oz (20 g) hacho miso (soybean
  miso), subsitute with aka miso
  (red miso)
1 teaspoon sugar
2/3 oz (20 g) walnuts, lightly roasted and
  chopped

Pickled mustard greens filling
1 teaspoon vegetable oil
1 teaspoon Korean virgin sesame oil
2 oz (60 g) takana (pickled mustard
  greens)
Pinch natural sea salt
Koikuchi shoyu (soy sauce)
3 teaspoons white sesame seeds, dry
  toasted until golden brown

At Shunju, we make a wide variety of pancakes and griddle cakes, the origins of which may be traced to Japanese okonomiyaki, Korean pancakes, and Italian foccacia. These recipes are for the latter; remember, the choice of stuffing is really up to you.

Basic dough recipe
1 Roll the dough on a floured surface with a rolling pin into a about 6 in (15 cm) in diameter. Place the filling in the center of the dough, lift up the sides of the dough and press together in the center so that the filling is enclosed in the dough. Roll the dough lightly into a ball.
2 Pour the sesame oil in a dish and roll the ball of dough so that it is completely coated. Place the ball in a heavy skillet over medium heat and place a flat-bottomed object, such as a saucepan on top of the ball so that it is flattened to about 3/4 in (2 cm) in thickness.
3 Grill until nicely browned and flip over. When both sides are nicely browned and crunchy, remove and cut into four wedges. Place on a warmed platter and serve immediately.

Prawn and garlic chive
1 Heat the vegetable oil in a saucepan over medium heat and lightly saute the prawns. Season with salt and pepper. When the prawns are lightly cooked, add the garlic chives and continue to sauté.
2 When the garlic chives become limp, add bonito stock and catsup and cook until the liquid has been reduced by half. Stir the dissolved starch and add to the saucepan. When the sauce is thickened, taste and correct seasoning if necessary. Empty the filling into a bowl.

Duck and walnut miso filling
1 Heat the vegetable oil in a saucepan over medium heat and sauté the duck. When the duck is browned, add mirin and bring to a full boil; boil off the alcohol content.
2 Reduce heat to low, add miso and sugar. Simmer until the sauce reduces and thickens.
3 Add the walnuts, mix well, and remove from heat. Empty the filling into a bowl.

Pickled mustard greens filling
1 Heat the vegetable and sesame oils in a saucepan and sauté pickled mustard greens over medium heat. Stir continuously with a wooden spatula scraping the bottom of the saucepan to prevent it from scorching. Add salt and soy sauce.
2 When all the liquid has evaporated, add some of the sesame seeds and remove from heat. Empty the filling into a bowl. Reserve the remaining sesame seeds to coat the dough ball later on.

Persimmon and meringue stacks
Kaki no mirufiyu jitate
柿のミルフィーユ仕立て

Serves 4
1 cup (250 ml) water
3 oz (90 g) sugar
3 1/2 tablespoons white dry wine
2 *kaki* (persimmons), about 10 oz
    (400 g), peeled, halved crosswise,
    deseeded and sliced crosswise into
    slices about 1/2 in (1 cm) thick to
    yield 8 slices
Scant 1/2 cup (100 ml) heavy (double)
    cream, whipped
2 egg whites
3 1/2 oz (100 g) brown sugar

The sweet variety of the Japanese persimmon, *kaki,* is a delicious fruit in comparison to the Western persimmon which has a tart, cheek-puckering flavor. The soft ripe persimmon and the crispy meringues create an interesting contrast of textures and a beautiful presentation. If you are blessed with the good fortune of having a persimmon tree in your garden, collect the brilliant red autumn leaves to garnish this dessert or to use as chopstick rests.

1 Preheat oven to 302°F (150°C, gas 2).
2 Combine the water, sugar, and wine in a saucepan and heat over medium heat until boiling. Remove from heat and cool. Pour into a container large enough to accommodate the persimmon slices, then add the persimmon and refrigerate for at least 2 hours.
3 Beat the egg whites until foamy with an electric mixer or by hand, gradually adding the brown sugar; continue beating until stiff peaks form. Spoon the meringue into a pastry bag.
4 Line a baking tray with parchment paper and squeeze eight circles about 2 in (5 cm) in diameter. Bake for about 10 minutes or until lightly browned and crispy. Turn off the oven and leave the meringues in the oven for about 2 hours to bake until crispy in the remaining heat. The baking is more of a drying than a heating process. Remove from oven and cool completely. Store in an airtight container until ready for assembly (can be stored up to one week).
5 To assemble, place a meringue in the center of a serving plate, spread on some whipped cream and top with the marinated persimmon. Place another meringue on top and layer again with cream and persimmon. Serve immediately.

Chestnut and green tea jellies

Kuri no nishoku mizu yokan

栗の二色水羊羹

Serves 4

1 lb 5 oz (600 g) fresh chestnuts, about 30 pieces, outer shells and inner skins discarded, soaked in water 15 minutes

Chestnut layer
6 oz (200 g) puréed chestnut
6 oz (200 g) granulated sugar
2/3 oz (20 g) stick *kanten* (gelatin made from red algae), about 2/3 stick, substitute with thread *kanten*, soaked in 1 2/3 cups (400 ml) water

Green tea layer
6 oz (200 g) puréed chestnut
6 oz (200 g) granulated sugar
2/3 oz (20 g) stick *kanten* (gelatin made from red algae), about 2/3 stick, substitute with thread *kanten*, soaked in 1 2/3 cups (400 ml) water
5 1/2 teaspoons *matcha* (powdered green tea) mixed with 4 teaspoons lukewarm water to form a paste
Pinch natural sea salt

We make a variety of *yokan*, naturally with flavors made with the ingredients which arrive with each season. As *yokan* is a very rich confection, the variety which we eat in the hot summer months is a lighter version called *mizu yokan*. Although this is an autumn dessert, we have made a *mizu yokan* which is more appealing to the modern calorie conscious society.

1 Place a steamer on high heat until steam starts to rise. Steam the peeled chestnuts for about 20 to 25 minutes over medium heat, until they are easily pierced with a fork or bamboo skewer. Purée the chestnuts with a spatula over a sieve.
2 Put the puréed chestnut, water, and sugar into a saucepan over medium heat. Stir the mixture continuously with a wooden spatula scraping the bottom of the saucepan to prevent it from catching. When it reaches a boil, lower the heat to low. Add a pinch of salt, squeeze the water out of the *kanten*, then tear it into small pieces and add it to the saucepan.
3 When *kanten* is completely melted, pour the mixture through a fine sieve and pour into *nagashigata* (square metal mold) and chill in the refrigerator. Can be substituted with a square, preferably metal, box about 15 cm square and at least 5 cm deep but without an insert, like a *nagashigata*, you will carefully have to slice along the edge to remove the finished dessert.
4 Repeat step 2 with the ingredients for the green tea layer. When *kanten* is completely melted, add the green tea paste and pour the mixture through a fine sieve. Cool to room temperature, and when the surface of the refrigerated mixture begins to firm, pour the green tea mixture over it. Refrigerate for 1 hour, then cut into 12 pieces.

Poached pears in wine

Nashi no konpoto

梨のコンポート

Serves 4
2 *nashi* (or other) pears, peeled, cut in half crosswise, cores and seeds removed
3/4 cup (200 ml) dry white wine
1 1/4 cups (300 ml) water
1/2 cup (120 g) sugar
1/2 vanilla bean (cut in half lengthwise)
Mint leaves to garnish

Nashi, or Japanese pear, has become very popular in the West in the past few years and can be found in many gourmet stores. It is mentioned in *Nihon Shoki*, the oldest record of Japanese history dating back to AD 720, but is presumed to have its origins in China where some similar varieties can be found. It is a delicious fruit, crispy in texture, similar to an apple, and much juicier than the Western pear with 88 percent water content. It is not only an autumn seasonal delicacy, but one of the favorite fruits of Japan.

1 Place the pears in a saucepan large enough to fit all the pear halves without overlapping. Pour the wine, water, sugar and vanilla bean over the pears and heat over medium heat until boiling. Lower the heat and poach until the pears can be easily pierced with a bamboo skewer. Remove from heat and cool. Refrigerate overnight in the cooking liquid.

2 Slice the pear halves into two and serve each slice with the cooking liquid and a mint leaf to garnish.

Plum wine jelly with kyoho grape

Kyoho iri umeshu zerii

巨峰入り梅酒ゼリー

Serves 4
1 1/4 cups (300 ml) *umeshu* (plum wine)
1/2 oz (15 g) sheet gelatin, soaked until softened
1/4 cup (50 g) superfine (castor) sugar
4 teaspoons cognac
8 *kyoho* grapes, substitute with Muscat or Campbell grapes, peeled and deseeded

At Shunju we take great pride in our homemade fruit and herb tonics and we have made this dessert using our *umeshu*, plum wine, which in reality is Japanese apricot macerated in a spirit called *shochu*. This plum wine should be aged and mellowed for at least three years otherwise the alcohol content will be too strong.

1 Pour plum wine into a heatproof glass or enameled saucepan with the softened gelatin and heat over medium heat until it reaches a temperature of 104°F (40°C). Stir the mixture continuously with a wooden spatula scraping the bottom of the saucepan to prevent it from scorching. Stir in the sugar when the gelatin is completely melted. Remove from heat and cool until 97°F (36°C).

2 Stir in the cognac, pour into a square mold, then add the grapes with even distance between them and refrigerate for 1 hour. When the gelatin begins to set, cover with plastic wrap and refrigerate 2 days.
3 Before serving, cut the jelly with a grapefruit spoon, to get a corrugated edge, with a grape in the center of each piece of jelly.

winter

The Shunju way of entertaining on a chilly winter's evening is to warm the body and soul with hearty dishes, good *sake* and even better company. We like to let our diners indulge themselves wholeheartedly by digging into steaming, sizzling, and bubbling seafood in a hot pot or on a charcoal grill. Among the seasonal specialties are blowfish, crabs, oysters and anglerfish, all of which we serve in simple, unpretentious styles.

An abundance of treasured gastronomical delights arrives with the winter season, such as *fugu* (blowfish), crabs, oysters, and *anko* (anglerfish). These ingredients are expensive and often served in a style which we find a bit pretentious. We like to prepare these ingredients using simple, unadorned cooking methods to let our diners indulge themselves wholeheartedly by digging into the steaming, sizzling or bubbling seafood in a hotpot or on a charcoal grill.

Nabe, hotpot, is an important winter dish in Japan. It is basically a hotpot meal cooked at the dining table on a charcoal brazier, *mizu konro*, or, more frequently in recent years, on a portable gas stove . The pot, normally earthenware, or in Shunju's case, hand-fashioned copper or ironware, is filled with a broth and ingredients, seafood or meat and vegetables, are cooked in the broth at the table. The flavor of the broth is enriched by the various ingredients, and the meal is often finished with *zosui*, a rice gruel cooked in the pot by adding rice or *udon* noodles and in some circumstances topped with beaten eggs and chopped green scallion.

Nabe not only acts as the centerpiece of the dining table and as a meal in one dish, but most importantly, also provides a perfect setting for family and friends to gather and chat. We even have an expression for this, "*nabe wo kakomu*," to gather around a *nabe* or "*nabe wo tsutsuku*," to pick at the *nabe* serving one selves and others directly from the *nabe*.

below left to right Pasta-like strips of *daikon* radish being added to our Oxtail Hotpot. A *nabe* dinner setting around the *ro*, charcoal pit, in Mishuku restaurant. *Mate gai*, a kind of shellfish, to be steamed in sake.

Korean-style Spicy Bouillabaisse Hotpot bubbling on the fire at the winter beach. Opposite Fresh *kinki* (a kind of red snapper), scallops, and squid bought directly from the port for our Korean-style Spicy Bouillabaisse Hotpot.

Oysters grilled on the half shelf

Yaki gaki

焼き牡蛎

Serves 4
8 unopened oysters in their shells
8 teaspoons *koikuchi shoyu* (soy sauce)
4 *sudachi*, halved, substitute with
  lemons

With the exception of the gigantic *iwa gaki* oyster that is a summer delicacy, all other oysters are eaten only in the winter in Japan and are therefore considered a winter delicacy along with crab. Since there are very few wild oysters left, they are farmed extensively throughout Japan with the most famous hailing from the Matoya farm in Hiroshima, where the history of oyster farming dates back to 1670. Japanese oysters are very large in comparison to those in America or Europe so you may want to serve more oysters per person.

1 Hold the oyster, deep shell down, in a folded washcloth or napkin in the palm of your left hand. Insert an oyster knife into the hinge of the shell. Gently turn the knife to pry open the upper shell enough to cut the hinge muscle. Once you have cut the muscle, slide the knife between the shells to open. The flesh should be attached to the deep shell. Discard the shallow shell and lightly rinse the deep shell with the flesh attached.
2 Grill on a charcoal grill in their shells. When the liquor released from the oysters begin to bubble, drizzle about 1 teaspoon soy sauce on each oyster.
3 Serve piping hot with *sudachi*.

Korean-style spicy bouillabaise hotpot

Kankoku-fu gyokai nabe

韓国風魚貝鍋

Serves 4
5 quarts (5 liters) water
1 squid, about 11 1/2 oz (350 g), cleaned (see Note)
2 medium *watari gani* (blue swimmer crabs), about 6 1/2 oz (200 g), substitute with dungeness or any other live crab or lobster, cleaned (see Note)
5 lb (2 1/2 kg) kinki (red snapper), substitute with any fatty, white flesh fish, cleaned, rinsed, and heads removed (follow steps 1 through 8 on page 244), cut crosswise into steaks
6 1/2 oz (200 g) oysters (serve 1 or more per person depending on size), shucked
1 1/2 lb (800 g) scallops in their shell (serve 1 or more per person depending on size), substitute with unshelled or frozen scallops
5 oz (150 g) *nagate ebi* (similar to Italian scampi), substitue with crawfish, slice in half lengthwise and devein
1 1/2 lb (1 1/2 lb (150 g) *hakusai* (Chinese cabbage), roughly chopped
5 oz (150 g) *mizuna* (pot herb mustard green), substitute with any mustard greens or other green leaf vegetable, roughly chopped
3 1/2 oz (100 g) *naga negi* (long welsh onion), substitute with white part of scallion (spring onion), roughly chopped

Seasonings
2 tablespoons Korean virgin sesame oil
1/3 cup (75 ml) *koikuchi shoyu* (soy sauce)
2 medium cloves garlic
2 tablespoons *kochujang* (Korean red chili paste), or to taste
1/2 teaspoon sugar
1 teaspoon Korean red pepper flakes

This is one of our most popular hotpot dishes and has been on our menu since we first opened. Korean cuisine has a spicy seafood hotpot called *maeuntang*. We have borrowed the idea from this dish to make our version of a spicy bouillabaisse. As with all our other hotpot recipes, this hotpot should be cooked at the dining table, and the vegetables added for each round of serving. Be sure to finish off this meal with rice or noodles cooked in this fabulous broth. Naturally, live seafood makes a more delicious hotpot but all the seafood listed here can be substituted with other varieties, and use frozen if it is difficult to obtain live ingredients.

1 Add the water and seafood to a large saucepan or stockpot and heat. When it reaches a hard boil, reduce the heat to low and simmer for 30 minutes or until the stock tastes rich. Skim off the foam that rises to the surface.
2 Combine all the seasoning ingredients and mix thoroughly. Adjust the red chili paste to taste. Add the seasoning to the pot.
3 Pour the stew into an earthenware or copper pot. Put the pot on the charcoal brazier or portable gas stove at the table. Adjust heat to low to maintain a strong simmer throughout the course of the meal.
4 Add half of the chopped Chinese cabbage, thicker bottom pieces first. When the cabbage is thoroughly cooked, add half of the *mizuna* and welsh onion and, as soon they have wilted, serve immediately divided into individual small bowls, or diners can serve themselves directly from the pot.

5 Repeat when diners are ready for their next round of portions. Don't forget to frequently skim off the foam that floats to the surface.

Note: To clean the squid, wash thoroughly under running water to remove the sliminess. Grasp the head section just below the eyes and pull the body away from the tail, fin and ink sac. Remove the ink saccarefully, taking care not to break it. Cut away the tentacles. Chop everything into bite size pieces.
To clean the crabs, wash thoroughly under running water. Grab the legs firmly with your left hand and pull the entire chest section free from the hard shell. Cut out and discard the feathery lung sections. Chop the legs off and chop the body into bite size pieces.

Oyster and fluffy tofu hotpot
Kaki to oboro dofu nabe
牡蠣とおばろ豆腐鍋

Serves 4
5 oz (150 g) shucked oysters
1/2 cup (80 g) grated *daikon* radish
10 oz (300 g) *hakusai* (Chinese cabbage), leaves cut into large squares, stem cut into long thin strips
5 stems *wakegi*, substitute with the green tops of scallion (spring onion), cut into 6-in (15-cm) lengths
6 cups (1 1/2 liters) *katsuo dashi* (bonito stock) (see page 248)
2 medium cloves garlic, minced
1 tablespoon *usukuchi shoyu* (light soy sauce)
Pinch natural sea salt
Generous grinding of black pepper

Tofu
2 cups + 2 tablespoons (540 ml) soy milk (see page 254)
2 teaspoons *nigari* (bittern), see page 53

There are many different versions of traditional hotpot made with oysters: especially popular are *dotenabe*, flavored with miso; or *mizore*, cooked with grated *daikon* radish. This original version is inspired by a spicy Korean tofu stew made with short-necked clams. If you are not too keen on oysters, experiment with other shellfish.

1 Prepare the tofu according to the recipe for basic homemade tofu on page 207.
2 Place the oysters in a bowl with the grated radish and mix gently to clean the oysters. Wash with water and drain.
3 Arrange the cut vegetables, tofu (carefully lifted out with a slotted spoon), and the oysters aesthetically on a large platter or flat, circular basket or lacquer tray.
4 Pour the bonito stock into an earthenware or copper pot. Transfer the pot to a charcoal brazier or portable gas stove at the table. Add soy sauce and garlic, and season with salt and pepper. Bring to a boil over medium heat. Reduce heat to low to maintain a strong simmer throughout the course of the meal.
5 To the simmering broth add first the oysters, then the vegetables and finally the tofu, about one-quarter at a time. Do not overcook the ingredients. Repeat when diners are ready for their next round of portions.
6 Serve immediately divided into individual small bowls, or diners can serve themselves directly from the pot. Frequently skim off the foam which floats to the surface. Garlic and black pepper can be added though the course of the dinner. We like to add lots of black pepper!

Crabs baked in sea salt crust

Kani no shio gama

かにの塩釜

Serves 4

6 lb (3 kg) natural sea salt
2 egg whites
1 live *ke gani* (horse-hair crab), about 1 1/2 lb (750 g), rinsed well and drained
1 live *watari gani* (blue swimmer crab), about 1 1/2 lb (750 g), rinsed well and drained
8 bamboo grass leaves, substitute with *wakame* seaweed (or any natural seaweed collected on the beach if you're cooking crabs at the beach)
2 *sudachi*, halved, substitute with lemons

In this recipe, crabs are roasted in a paste made from natural sea salt and egg white. We often use this method of cooking for seafood which, we presume, evolved from the traditional *hamayaki* (seafood grilled on hot rocks at the beach) of the Inland Sea region. Sea bream would be placed on a bed of hot sea salt, then covered with more salt and steamed in straw. The salt absorbs steam and forms a hard crust as it bakes, sealing in the moisture and flavor. When the crust is cracked open, it reveals a crab so sweet and pure it tastes as if it was just caught from the sea. Japanese crabs are quite a different species from the Western crabs. The most coveted are horse-hair crabs (*ke gani*), indigenous to Hokkaido, and Pacific snow crabs, known as *matsuba gani* or *echizen gani* depending on where they are caught. Blue swimmer crab (*watari gani*) is more readily available and also delicious. You can use any variety of live crab or lobster for this recipe.

1 Preheat oven to 338°F (170°C, gas 3 1/2) or, if cooking outdoors, prepare the coals in a kettle-type barbecue grill (you need the lid to make this recipe).
2 Put the salt in a large bowl with the egg white and mix with your hands until it becomes foamy and fluffy.
3 Wrap the crabs with the bamboo grass leaves.
4 Spread one-quarter of the salt mixture on a baking sheet and place the crabs on top. Cover completely with the remaining salt mixture.
5 Bake for 40 to 50 minutes. When the salt forms a hard crust, remove from the oven and pierce through the crust and into a crab with a metal skewer to test for doneness. Remove the metal skewer 5 seconds later, and if the skewer is warmed to about 104°F/40°C (hot, but not too hot to touch), the crabs are cooked. If the metal skewer is not hot enough, return it to the oven, lower the temperature to 302°F (150°C, gas 2) and cook for a further 10 minutes, and repeat the testing.
6 Place the baked salt crust on a wooden cutting board and crack it open with a hammer. Serve in its crust garnished with *sudachi*.

Winter starters

Fuyu no otoshi

冬のお通し

Serves 4

Puréed green lily root balls (*yuri ne no oribe dango*)

13 oz (400 g) *yuri ne* (lily root), washed and broken into layers (discard any discolored layers)
Scant 1/2 cup (100 ml) water
4 teaspoons heavy (double) cream
1 teaspoon superfine (castor) sugar
10 teaspoons *macha* (powdered green tea)
Pinch natural sea salt

1 In a saucepan, bring lily root and water to a boil over medium heat, reduce heat and simmer for 2 minutes. Drain and cool.
2 Purée the boiled lily root in a sieve and divide into two bowls.
3 Add cream and half of the sugar to one bowl, mix well. Add the powdered green tea, salt and remaining sugar to the other bowl and mix well.
4 Divide both mixtures into 2/3 oz (20 g) portions and roll them into balls. Press 1 green and 1 white ball together, and roll them into 1 ball. Pinch the top portion of the ball with your fingers. Serve.

Steamed duck rolled with onion (*mushi gamo no negi maki*)

1 duck breast, fat discarded, flesh scored 2 in (5 cm) apart
1 2/3 cups (400 ml) *katsu dashi* (bonito stock) (see page 248)
2 tablespoons *koikuchi shoyu* (soy sauce)
2 tablespoons *mirin*
Pinch grated ginger
1/2 *naga negi* (long welsh onion), substitute with white part of scallion (spring onion), sliced into matchstick slivers

1 Heat a skillet over high heat and brown the skin side of the duck first. When nicely browned, flip and brown the other side. Move the skillet constantly so that the duck does not stick and burn.
2 Mix all the ingredients except for the *naga negi* (or scallion) in a shallow bowl, add the browned duck, cover with plastic wrap, and steam over high heat for 15 minutes.
3 Remove the duck from the liquid and reserve. Cool the liquid (place the bowl in iced water) and when the fat begins to solidify, strain through a sieve and return the duck to the liquid. Marinate the duck for 3 hours.
4 Wipe off any excess liquid, slice the duck thinly and roll with the *negi*.

Squid rolled with spicy cod roe (*ika no mentai maki*)

3 1/2 oz (100 g) *mentaiko* (spicy cod roe), available frozen in Japanese grocery stores
1 sashimi-quality squid, 5 oz or 150 g without the head and tentacles, cleaned and skinned

1 Make an incision in the thin membrane of the cod roe and squeeze the roe out by running the dull side of your knife along the membrane.
2 Cut the squid lengthwise into strips about 2 in (5 cm) thick but do not cut through the entire length; stop about one-third of the way up, leaving the upper portion as one piece.
3 Place the squid sideways on your cutting board and spread the cod roe evenly. Roll the squid away from you.

When tightly rolled, wrap in plastic wrap and place in the freezer until half-frozen. Slice into 1-cm thick rolls.

Blanched chrysanthemum leaves (*shungiku no nibitashi*)

2 *aburaage* (deep-fried thin tofu slices)
10 stalks *shungiku* (chrysanthemum leaves), substitute with spinach or dandelion greens, blanched and refreshed in iced water
2 *kanpyo* (dried gourd) strings
2 cups (540 ml) *katsuo dashi* (bonito stock) (see page 248)
2 tablespoons *koikuchi shoyu* (soy sauce)
2 tablespoons *mirin*

1 Place tofu slices on a basket or in a sieve and pour some boiling water over them to remove the oil. Cut open to make a flat square, then cut the chrysanthemum leaves to the same length. Place the leaves on the tofu and roll. Tie the roll in six places using the gourd strips.
2 Place all the ingredients in a saucepan together with the tofu rolls and bring to a boil over medium heat. When it reaches a boil remove from heat and cool. Let the roll marinate in the liquid for 1 hour.
3 Wipe off any excess liquid, then slice each roll into six pieces so that the tie lies in the middle of each sliced section.

Note: All dishes are served at room temperature.

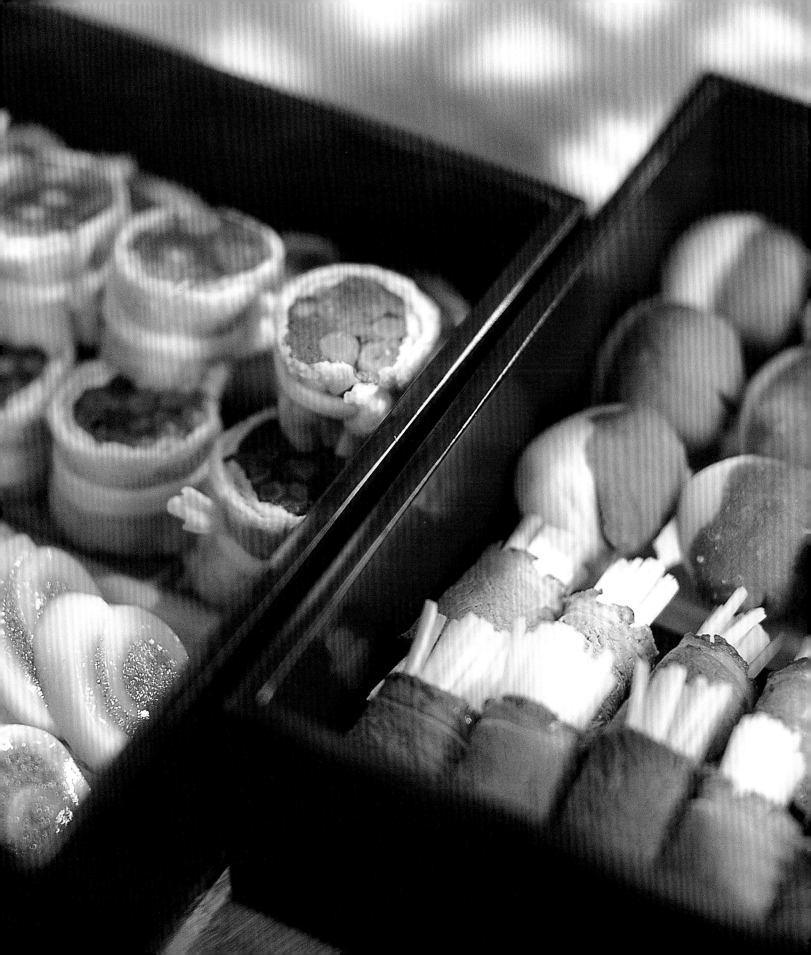

Freshly made hotpot tofu
On dofu
温豆腐

Serves 4
1 2/3 cups (400 ml) homemade soymilk
(see page 254)
2 teaspoons natural *nigari* (bittern), see
Note page 53

Condiments
2 1/2 tablespoons *banno negi*, substitute with scallions (spring onions),
finely sliced
5 g *zasai* (salty Chinese pickled root
vegetable), minced
2 tablespoons *ito gaki* (extra thin bonito
shavings)
Shiro shoyu (white soy sauce), substitue
with *usukuchi shoyu* (light soy sauce)
2/3 oz (20 g) *aka* miso (red miso)
1/3 clove garlic, minced

Tofu has always been a favorite food of the Japanese. Penned during the Edo Period (17th to 18th century), *Tofu Hyakuchin* (One Hundred Tofu) is a compilation of tofu recipes that was cherished by all, from the feudal lords to the masses. As the title suggests, tofu has a wide range of applications. Of course the ultimate delight is in savoring freshly made tofu, either piping hot or chilled, as an appetizer or a main dish, or to complement *sake*. One can eat it every day without being bored of its taste, and it is recognized internationally as one of the most important health foods of our day. This recipe was our first homemade tofu dish. We make this dish in a covered earthenware hot pot, made by a kiln called Doraku, on a charcoal brazier or on a portable gas stove at the dining table in front of our guests. There is nothing more delightful than waiting for the tofu to solidify. When you use our recipe for making the soymilk, the tofu is so rich and sweet in flavor that it makes you want to eat it without any sauce or condiments but if you do eat it with soy sauce, we recommend you use white soy sauce or natural sea salt since it will not stain the beautiful tofu. This recipe makes one hotpot about 8 in (20 cm) in diameter.

1 Place the finely sliced scallion, pickled root vegetable, bonito shavings and soy sauce in separate bowls. Mix the miso and garlic and place in a bowl.
2 Prepare the basic soymilk recipe (page 254) by following steps 1 through 8.
3 Place soymilk into an earthenware pot over low heat stirring with a wooden or bamboo ladle scraping the bottom to prevent from scorching. When the temperature reaches 167°F (75°C)—normally in about 7 or 8 minutes—turn off the heat. Pour in the bittern.
4 Stir the soymilk and bittern with a wooden or bamboo spoon.
5 Cover. Tofu should solidifiy in 5 minutes. Serve immediately in the hot pot along with condiments and white soy sauce. Tofu will become tough if it is over heated.

Yam and turnip hotpot
Tsukune imo to kyo kabu no mizore nabe
つくね芋と京蕪のみぞれ鍋

Serves 4
Scant 1/2 cup (100 ml) chicken broth,
  preferably homemade
1 teaspoon natural sea salt
4 cups (1 liter) *katsuo dashi* (bonito
  stock) (see page 248)
4 oz (130 g) chicken breast, cut into
  3/4-in (1 1/2-cm) chunks
12 oz (375 g) grated *tsukune imo* (a kind
  of yam), substitute with *yama imo*
  (yam) or *nagaimo* (Chinese yam)
6 oz (180 g) grated *kyo kabu* (Kyoto
  turnip)
6 1/2 oz (200 g) *kyo kabu* (Kyoto turnip),
  substitute with 3 regular turnips or
  daikon, scrubbed thoroughly until skin
  is smooth, skin lightly peeled off, then
  sliced into 12 paper thin slices
2 thick *shimonita negi* (Shimonita leeks),
  substitute with Western leeks, outer
  skin removed, washed and grit
  removed, cut diagonally into 2-in
  (5-cm) pieces
10 oz (300 g) *mizuna* (pot herb mustard),
  substitute with spinach, soaked in several changes of cold water, drained
  and cut in half
3 1/2 oz (100 g) *fugu negi* (welsh or
  ciboule onion), substitute with green
  stalks of thin scallions (spring onions),
  soaked in several changes of cold
  water, drained

Kyoto is renowned for its own kind of vegetables, the majority of which are winter root vegetables. The *kyo kabu* or *shogoin kabura* is much larger and firmer than the normal Japanese turnip, weighing up to 10 lb (5 kg) and growing as large as a baby's head. The *tsukune imo* yam is round whereas other Japanese yams are either glove-shaped or long. The name *mizore* means sleet since the grated turnip and yam is fluffy and white, resembling snow. You can make this recipe with grated *daikon* radish if it is difficult to obtain Japanese turnips.

1 Combine the chicken broth, sea salt, and bonito stock.
2 Add chicken breast chunks and lightly braise the chicken over medi-um heat, about 5 minutes. Allow the broth and chicken to cool to room temperature.
3 Arrange the vegetables on a large platter, or flat, circular basket or lacquer tray.
4 To prevent discoloring, just before adding the *tsukune imo* yam to the broth, peel off the skin (carefully, as it is very slippery) and grate. Add the grated *kyo kabu* and *tsukune imo* yam a little at a time to the broth and simultaneously whip the broth with a whisk so that the grated vegetables are thoroughly incorpo-rated into the broth.

5 Pour the broth into the earthen-ware, or copper, pot. Put the pot on the charcoal brazier or portable gas stove at the table. Adjust heat to low heat to maintain a strong simmer throughout the course of the meal.
6 Add vegetables to the simmering broth, about 1/4 at a time. The veg-etables should be blanched shortly. Do not overcook the vegetables. Repeat when diners are ready for their next round of portions. Serve immediately divided into individual small bowls, or diners can serve themselves directly from the pot. Frequently skim off the foam, which floats to the surface.

Root vegetable dumpling soup

Konsai no suiton

根菜のすいとん

Serves 4

4 oz (120 g) *kabocha* (Japanese pumpkin), substitute with Western pumpkin, peeled and grated

4 oz (120 g) *gobo* (burdock root), peeled and grated

4 oz (120 g) carrots, peeled and grated

4 oz (120 g) daikon, peeled and grated

5 1/2 oz (160 g) *yamato imo* (Japanese yam), substitute with taro, peeled and grated

1 tablespoon *katakuri* starch, substitute with potato starch

3/4 cup (200 ml) *katsuo dashi* (bonito stock) (see page 248)

1 teaspoon *mirin*

1 teaspoon *usukuchi shoyu* (light soy sauce)

Pinch natural sea salt

12 in (30 cm) square of *rishiri konbu* (kelp), soaked in water until tender

15 stalks *mizuna* (pot herb mustard), substitute with spinach

10 Korean red chili pepper threads

This is a beautiful dish as well as an extremely healthy one, full of dietary fiber from the root vegetables. It is a perfect dish to serve to vegetarians or the calorie conscious. You will need a wire basket to hold the kelp, which is actually the serving dish. If you don't have a wire basket, you can use some chicken wire to fashion your own, or try using a metal mesh sieve.

1 Place the grated Japanese pumpkin, burdock root, carrots, and *daikon* in individual bowls then add 1/3 oz (10 g) grated yam and a pinch of starch to each bowl. Mix well until each feels soft and doughy. Roll each grated vegetable into bite-sized balls then flatten slightly in the palm of your hand.

2 Place bonito stock, *mirin*, soy sauce, and salt in a saucepan and heat over medium heat until it reaches boiling. Lower the heat, add the vegetable dumplings, and braise lightly.

3 Place *konbu* in a wire basket small enough so that the sides of the kelp come up to hold the hot liquid. Gently place the dumplings and broth into the kelp, add the *mizuna* and garnish with red pepper threads. Serve immediately.

Oxtail hotpot
Gyu teiru nabe
牛テール鍋

Serves 4
Scant 1 cup (200 ml) oxtail soup (see recipe below)
4 cups (1 liter) *katsuo dashi* (bonito stock) (see page 248)
3 1/3 tablespoons *mirin*
3 1/3 tablespoons *koikuchi shoyu* (soy sauce)
2 tablespoons milk
Pinch natural sea salt
1 lb 3 oz (600 g) *daikon*, washed and peeled, cut into long pasta-like strips (run a vegetable peeler lengthwise)
1 tablespoon Korean red chili pepper slivers

Oxtail soup
5 quarts (5 liters) water
1 teaspoon natural sea salt
2 lb (1 kg) oxtail, disjointed
5 quarts (5 liters) water
1 lb (500 g) onions, peeled and sliced
6 1/2 oz (200 g) carrots, peeled and sliced
5 oz (150 g) celery, peeled and sliced

This is one of our most popular hotpot dishes and has been on our menu since we first opened. Oxtail makes wonderfully rich soup and the light *daikon* pasta-like strips are a perfect match for this hearty soup. You can omit the red pepper if you do not care for spicy food. As with all our other hotpot recipes, this hotpot should be cooked at the dining table and the *daikon* added for each round of serving. Be sure that you finish off this meal with rice or noodles cooked in this fabulous broth.

1 To boil the oxtail, bring 5 quarts water and sea salt to a boil in a pot large enough to accommodate the oxtail. When the water reaches a full boil, add the oxtail. When the water returns to a boil, drain in a colander, and rinse the oxtail quickly under cold running water.
2 Add the fresh 5 quarts water and sliced vegetables to the pot and bring to a full boil. Add the oxtail. Lower the heat when it returns to a full boil and simmer until the oxtail is tender and easily removed from the bone, about 3 hours. Frequently skim off the foam that rises to the surface
3 Remove the oxtail from the pot and reserve. Strain the soup through a sieve to remove the vegetables.
4 Return the soup to the pot and bring to a full boil. Skim off excess fat from the surface. Strain through a fine sieve or through a cheesecloth. Reserve.

5 To prepare the hotpot, place the oxtail soup, bonito stock, *mirin*, and soy sauce into saucepan and bring to a boil over medium heat. Add the oxtail, when it returns to a boil, add the milk and season with salt.
6 Pile *daikon* strips on a platter and garnish with red pepper slivers.
7 Pour the soup into the earthenware or copper pot. Put the pot on the charcoal brazier or portable gas stove at the table. Adjust heat to low heat to maintain a strong simmer throughout the course of the meal. Add *daikon* to the simmering soup, about one-quarter at a time. Repeat when diners are ready for their next round of portions. The *daikon* should be tender. Serve immediately divided into individual small bowls, or diners can serve themselves directly from the pot. Frequently skim off the foam that floats to the surface.

Chicken meatball hotpot

Tsukune nabe

つくね鍋

Serves 4
4 lb (2 kg) chicken bones, thoroughly
  rinsed
3 quarts (3 liters) water
2 teaspoons *usukuchi shoyu* (light soy
  sauce)
4 teaspoons *sake*
1 teaspoon natural sea salt (optional)
8 oz (240 g) finely minced free-range
  chicken
1 2/3 oz (50 g) *naga negi* (long welsh
  onion), substitute with white part of
  scallion (spring onion), finely chopped
1/2 *yuzu* (Japanese citron), about 2 oz
  (60 g), grated or find the dried, powdered peel sold in Japanese grocery
  stores, omit if unavailable
Pinch natural sea salt
Pinch freshly ground black pepper
1 block tofu, about 10 oz (300 g), sliced
  into 8 blocks
5 oz (150 g) *mizuna* (pot herb mustard),
  substitute with spinach

This is one of our most popular hotpot dishes and has been on our menu since we first opened. *Tsukune* are finely minced meatballs of fish, poultry, or meat and are either grilled, as is done in *yakitori* restaurants, or made into a hotpot dish. The chicken broth plays a crucial part in this dish so we ask that you take the time to make it from scratch. As with all our other hotpot recipes, this hotpot should be cooked at the dining table and the *mizuna* added for each round of serving. Be sure that you finish off this meal with rice or noodles cooked in this delicious broth!

1 Place the chicken bones and water in a large stockpot and bring to a boil over medium heat. When it reaches a hard boil, reduce the heat to low and simmer for 3 to 4 hours. Frequently skim off the foam that rises to the surface. Strain through a fine sieve or cheesecloth.
2 Add soy sauce and *sake*; add salt if necessary. Set aside.
3 Knead the minced chicken and chopped *naga negi* thoroughly with your hands, then add the grated citron peel, salt, and pepper. Divide into 8 portions and roll into balls. An alternative is to spread it flat on a large leaf to spoon into the pot at the table.
4 Pour the chicken broth into an earthenware or copper pot. Put the pot on a charcoal brazier or portable gas stove at the table. Adjust the heat to low heat to maintain a strong simmer throughout the course of the meal. Add the meat-balls to the simmering broth, 4 at a time. When they float to the surface they are cooked.
5 Add the tofu. When the tofu is warmed thoroughly, add *mizuna* and, as soon it has wilted, serve by dividing into individual small bowls, or diners can serve themselves directly from the pot. Repeat when diners are ready for their next round of portions. Frequently skim off the foam that floats to the surface.

Cauliflower mousse

Kalifulawa no musu

カリフラワーのムース

Serves 4

1 medium cauliflower (800 g), broken into florets, stalk and leaves discarded
1/2 potato, peeled and thinly sliced
3 oz (90 ml) heavy (double) cream
Pinch natural sea salt
Pinch white pepper
4 teaspoons caviar

Although this is not a tofu recipe, we have included it with the Soymilk Film and Sea Urchin with Jellied Consommé Sauce recipe as they can both be easily prepared in advance and complement one another as beautiful appetizers for a large dinner party.

1 Simmer the cauliflower and potato in a saucepan until tender when pierced with a fork. Drain and transfer to a food processer. Purée the cauliflower and potato with the cream and season. If the purée is too thick, add some milk, a tablespoon at a time to yield a fluffy mousse. Taste and correct for seasoning. Cool.
2 Spoon the cauliflower mousse into cocktail glasses and top with caviar. Top with caviar at the last moment as it will stain the mousse.

Soymilk yuba and sea urchin with jellied consommé sauce

Nama yuba no uni jule gake

生湯葉の雲丹ジュレ掛け

Serves 4

3/4 cup (200 ml) *katsuo dashi* (bonito stock) (see page 248)
2 tablespoons *koikuchi shoyu* (soy sauce)
5 teaspoons *mirin*, alcohol boiled off to yield about 4 teaspoons
Pinch natural sea salt
Handful *kezuibushi* (dried bonito shavings)
2 sheet gelatin, soaked until soft
3 1/2 oz (100 g) *yuba* (soymilk film), see page 255 (make without green beans, only with soymilk), can be prepared 1 day in advance
1 1/3 oz (40 g) fresh *uni* (sea urchin) fllesh
1 fresh wasabi root, grated, substitute with frozen fresh or tube wasabi

This is a completely different way to enjoy soymilk film, a variation on the orthodox recipe with soy sauce and wasabi. Try this recipe with the rich taste of fresh sea urchin. They both have a very creamy consistency and complement one another well.

1 Combine bonito stock, soy sauce, mirin, and salt in a saucepan and heat over medium heat. Remove from heat just before boiling and add bonito shavings. When the bonito shavings sink to the bottom, immediately strain through a fine sieve lined with *sarashi* (a kind of cheesecloth) or paper towel.
2 Return the stock to a boil, remove from heat and add the softened gelatin, stirring with a spatula. When the gelatin is thoroughly incorporated into the stock, pour into a bowl set in a larger bowl filled with iced water until the gelatin thickens. This can be done a few hours in advance and chilled in the refrigerator.
3 To assemble, spoon soymilk film into cocktail glasses, top with sea urchin, then arrange the jellied sauce on the very top. Garnish with a dab of grated wasabi.

Vinegar-marinated pacific mackerel sashimi

Shime saba

〆鯖

Serves 4

Handful natural sea salt

1 lb 3 oz (600 g) sashimi-quality mackerel, cut in three-section fillet (see page 244), pelvic bone sliced off

1 sheet *konbu* (kelp), about 4 in (10 cm) square, gently wiped clean (leaving the flavorful white powder on the *konbu*)

Su (rice vinegar)

7 teaspoons fresh wasabi, grated, substitute with frozen fresh or tube wasabi

Several wasabi leaves, omit, or substitute with any beautiful leaf

Koikuchi shoyu (soy sauce)

Saba, Pacific mackerel, is best eaten in late autumn and early winter when its fat content increases to 15%. It is a spectacular blue-green fish with distinctive markings on its back. As the fish is very oily, it is usually grilled or braised but the most luxurious way to enjoy it must be to marinate it in vinegar and *konbu*. This is actually a traditional method of preservation to transport the raw fish wrapped in grass bamboo leaves to the feudal lords living far inland. There is even an old route referred to as *saba kaido*.

1 Spread the salt evenly in a flat container, large enough to accommodate the mackerel, so that the bottom is completely covered with salt.

2 Place the filleted mackerel on the salt, skin-side down, and cover completely with salt. Leave in a cool place for 3 to 4 hours, depending on the oiliness of the fish.

3 Remove the mackerel from the salt, rinse the salt off under running water and pat dry. Wash the container.

4 Place *konbu* in the container, place the mackerel on top, and pour enough vinegar to cover the mackerel completely. Marinate for 1 hour.

5 Remove fish from marinade and remove the fine bones with tweezers.

6 Place the mackerel on a cutting board, skin-side up. Gently holding the fillet with your left hand, pull only the outer thin skin off (being careful not to break the flesh) from the head side.

7 Place the fillet on your cutting board skin-side up, make a deep incision in the center of the skin, about 3/4 in (1 1/2 cm) from the edge, and slice one piece, about 1 1/4 in (3 cm) thick so that the incision is in the center of each slice.

8 Arrange the slices aesthetically on the serving platter; place wasabi on the serving dish. Garnish with wasabi (or other) leaves and serve with soy sauce in individual dishes.

Yellowtail sashimi with pomegranate dressing

Buri no zakuro doreshingu
鰤のザクロドレッシング

Serves 4
1 1/4 cups (300 ml) water
2 teaspoons natural sea salt
2 tablespoons (10 g) powdered kelp,
    dissolved in hot water to make a kind
    of tea
10 oz (320 g) sashimi-quality filleted
    yellow tail, cut in *sori giri* cut (see
    page 247)
5 oz (125 g) *kyo kabu* or *shogoin kabura*
    (giant Kyoto turnip), substitute with
    turnip or *daikon*

Pomegranate dressing
1/4 pomegranate, divide into individual
    seeds, reserve half and process half
    into juice
1/2 cup (120 ml) vegetable oil
Juice of 1/2 lemon
Pinch natural sea salt

Buri, or yellowtail, is a favorite winter fish and is highly prized for its fatty flesh. It can be eaten as sashimi, grilled, or braised. We think that the pomegranate dressing not only gives this dish its beautiful ruby color, but the tartness of the fruit also suits the fatty yellowtail well. *Senmaizuke* is the famous pickle from Kyoto made with this giant turnip, *konbu* (kelp), and salt. The largest turnips are used for this pickle and are actually sliced with the traditional carpenter's planing tool in order to maintain the identical thickness of each slice. We have discovered that the powdered kelp works very well in making an instant version of this pickle.

1 Mix the water, salt, and powdered kelp in flat container. Slice the giant turnip crosswise into 3/4-in- (2-cm-) thick slices. Pickle the slices in the kelp mixture for about 1 hour. You should have enough slices to sandwich the yellow tail slices.
2 Whisk the vegetable oil, lemon, and salt with the pomegranate juice.

3 Drain the pickled giant turnips and wipe off any excess moisture. Sandwich slices of yellowtail sashimi between two slices of turnip. If using giant turnip, quarter each sandwiched piece. If normal turnip or *daikon*, you do not need to cut. Arrange on the serving platter, pour the dressing, and garnish with the reserved pomegranate seeds.

Braised winter vegetables

Fuyu yasai no taki awase

冬野菜炊き合せ

Serves 4

8 oz (250 g) *kyo kabu* or *shogoin kabura* (giant Kyoto turnip), substitute with turnip or *daikon*, scrubbed until smooth, lightly peeled and cut into 8 wedges

8 oz (250 g) *kyo ninjin* (Kyoto carrot), peeled and cut into 3/4-in (1 1/2-cm) slices

4 *kabu* (Japanese turnips), about 6 1/2 oz (200 g), peeled into a hexagonal shape and a cross incision made at the bottom

7 cups (1 3/4 liters) *katsuo dashi* (bonito stock) (see page 248)

3/4 cup (180 ml) *usukuchi shoyu* (light soy sauce)

Pinch natural sea salt

3/4 cup (180 ml) *mirin*

5 oz (150 g) *mizuna* (pot-herb mustard), substitute with spinach

Yuzu (Japanese citron) peel, substitute with lemon peel or omit, to garnish

8 *kinome* (young *sansho* leaves), optional

Traditionally, before the invention of greenhouse farming, only root vegetables were available during the long winter months. Kyoto is renowned for its unique vegetables, the majority of which are winter root vegetables. *Kyo ninjin*, or Kyoto carrot, has a much stronger flavor and color than the normal variety, and *shogoin kabura* or *kyo kabu* (giant Kyoto turnip) is much larger than the normal variety of *kabu*.

1 Slice the Kyoto turnip wedges crosswise in half if it is a large turnip. Slide your knife along the edges of the wedge at a 45 degree angle to shave off the sharp edge (this prevents the edges from disintegrating while braising). Shave off the edges of the Kyoto carrot slices in a similar fashion.

2 Combine the bonito stock, soy sauce, salt, and *mirin* and set aside scant 1 1/2 cups (360 ml) to be used in step 3. Divide the rest to braise each of the root vegetables separately until they can be easily pierced with a skewer.

3 Meanwhile, briefly blanch *mizuna*, refresh in cold water and soak in the reserved bonito stock mixture.

4 When all the vegetables have been braised, arrange in a serving bowl along with the *mizuna*, taking care not to damage the tender vegetables. Pour some of the hot broth and garnish with slivers of citron peel and young prickly ash leaves. Serve immediately. This recipe can be served hot or at room temperature.

Grilled daikon radish
Daikon no ippon yaki
大根の一本焼き

Serves 2
1 1/3 cups (360 ml) *katsuo dashi* (bonito stock) (see page 248)
1/3 cup (90 ml) chicken broth
Pinch natural sea salt
1 small organically grown *daikon* radish with leaves, about 8 in (20 cm) long, scrubbed under cold running water until smooth, leaves cut off and reserved
Pinch Korean large red pepper flakes

This popular winter dish was inspired by a small *daikon* radish that turned up in the kitchen one day. Yamazaki-san, our trusted farmer, had sent us radishes that were thinned out from the *daikon* patch. These would normally be thrown out in a conventional farm for being substandard but, in fact, they are delicious. They possess a concentrated flavor, and the smaller size allows us to grill them whole. This recipe absolutely requires an organically grown small firm daikon. No substitutes please!

1 Put bonito stock, chicken broth and natural sea salt into a pot and slowly braise the prepared *daikon* over low heat until it is very tender when pricked with a thin skewer or tooth-pick. Remove with a slotted spoon.
2 Briefly braise *daikon* leaves in the remaining broth. Set aside.
3 Broil braised *daikon* on a fish grill or steak skillet (skillet with ridges) until it is browned nicely with "broil lines".

4 Slice *daikon* slightly diagonally into 3/4 in (2 cm) slices and arrange on a dish to form its original shape. Cut the leaves into lengths of 2 in (5 cm) and arrange next to the braised daikon. Place a pinch of natural sea salt and Korean large red pepper flakes on tiny bowls (such as *sake* cups) or saucers and place on the dish with the *daikon*.

Anglerfish liver and braised daikon with glazed sauce

Ankimo to daikon no ankake

あん肝と大根のあんかけ

Serves 4
4 oz (120 g) thick *daikon* radish, peeled and cut into 2-in (5-cm) slices
1 tablespoon rice
3/4 cup (200 ml) *katsuo dashi* (bonito stock) (see page 248)
2 tablespoons *koikuchi shoyu* (soy sauce)
2 tablespoons *mirin*
1 2/3 oz (50 g) *ankimo* (fresh anglerfish liver), substitute with the steamed variety sold in cans
1 tablespoon *sake*
4 *banno negi*, substitute with grren tops of scallions (spring onions), finely chopped crosswise

Glazed sauce
1 3/4 cups (360 ml) *katsuo dashi* (bonito stock) (see page 248)
8 teaspoons (40 ml) *koikuchi shoyu* (soy sauce)
6 teaspoons (30 ml) tablespoons *mirin*
2 tablespoons (30 ml) *katakuri* starch, substitute with potato starch, dissolved in 2 tablespoons water

Anko, anglerfish, is an extremely ugly and devilish looking fish but it is extremely delicious and is considered a winter delicacy. The liver, *ankimo*, is highly coveted as a gourmet food and is often served in expensive establishments as an appetizer with *ponzu* sauce. It is very rich and is in many ways comparable to the French *foie gras*.

1 Slide a knife along the edge of both sides of the *daikon* slices at a 45 degree angle to shave off any sharp edges. This prevents the edges from disintegrating while braising the *daikon*. Place in a saucepan with just enough water to cover all of the slices and add 1 tablespoon rice. Simmer over low heat for 30 minutes. The rice prevents *daikon* from becoming discolored and produces a nice white color.
2 Put bonito stock, soy sauce, and *mirin* in a saucepan over high heat. When it boils, reduce the heat to low. Add the braised *daikon* and simmer for 20 minutes.
3 If you are using fresh anglerfish liver, remove the thin membrane taking care not to crush the liver. Sprinkle with *sake* and reserve for about 20 minutes. Omit this step if you are using canned *ankimo*.

5 Slice *ankimo* in four. Slice braised *daikon* in half crosswise and sandwich *ankimo* between the two halves. Place in a steamer and steam over high heat for 10 minutes.
6 Meanwhile, to make the sauce, put *katsuo dashi*, *mirin*, and soy sauce in a saucepan over high heat. Lower the heat to medium when it boils. Stir in the starch water a little at a time, checking the consistency so that it does not become clumpy or too thick. You may need less or more of the starch. Remove from heat.
7 Place the braised *daikon* into individual lacquer bowls, pour the hot glazed sauce and garnish with finely chopped *banno negi* or scallion.

Chinese cabbage with cashew nut sauce

Hakusai salada

白菜サラダ

Serves 2
1/4 medium-sized (200 g) hakusai
  (Chinese cabbage)
1/2 cup (100 g) cashew nuts
1 teaspoon sugar
2 teaspoons (10 g) *do ban jang* (Chinese
  fermented bean paste)
1 teaspoon natural sea salt
1/3 cup (90 ml) *katsuo dashi* (bonito
  stock) (see page 248)

Daikon radish and Chinese cabbage are the most common kinds of produce that come from the Yamazaki farm in winter. You may have eaten *shabu shabu* in a Japanese restaurant in which Chinese cabbage plays an integral part. There is normally a choice of *ponzu* sauce (citrus spiked soy sauce) and sesame dipping sauce. We find that the nutty flavor works well with Chinese cabbage and have come up with this cashew nut sauce. This is an extremely easy dish to make and you may want to make extra cashew sauce to keep in your refrigerator as it works well with many blanched vegetables.

1 Make a cut lengthwise from the base of the cabbage.
2 Toast the cashew nuts in a skillet until lightly browned, then set aside to cool.
3 Put the cashew nuts in a mortar and pestle and grind finely, or process in a food processor, until finely ground.

4 Blanch the cabbage. Drain, taking care to preserve its shape. Cut off the stem and cut crosswise into 2-in (5-cm) widths. Arrange the cut cabbage on a dish to form its original shape. Spoon the cashew sauce on the Chinese cabbage diagonally or sandwich in between the layers of leaves.

Pickled mustard greens fried rice

Takana meshi

高菜飯

Serves 4
2 tablespoons vegetable oil
2 oz (60 g) *takana* (pickled mustard greens), finely chopped
1 teaspoon white sesame seeds
2 1/2 cups (400 g) cold cooked rice
4 teaspoons *koikuchi shoyu* (soy sauce)
Pinch natural sea salt

Takana, pickled mustard greens, is typical of the heavily salted pickled vegetables that were preserved for the long, cold winters in Nagano Prefecture.

1 Heat the vegetable oil in a skillet over medium heat and lightly fry the chopped mustard greens. Add the sesame seeds and continue to fry until fragrant.
2 Add the cold rice to the skillet and stir constantly to avoid the rice from sticking to the pan. Fry the rice until it is slightly browned and evenly coated with mustard greens and sesame seeds. Drizzle the soy sauce onto the edge of the pan—not directly on the rice—to get a nice pungent fragrance. Add salt to taste.

Japanese-style omelet

Ji tamago yaki

地玉子焼き

Serves 4
Scant 2 cups (480 ml) *katsuo dashi*
  (bonito stock) (see page 248)
2 tablespoons *koikuchi shoyu* (soy
  sauce)
1 teaspoon sugar
Pinch natural sea salt
1 tablespoon *mirin*
12 free-range chicken eggs, lightly
  beaten with chopsticks
Vegetable oil
3 oz (90 g) *daikon* radish, grated and
  excess liquid drained

Tamago yaki is among one of the most popular dishes in Japan. It can be made in a variety of ways and served either hot or cold, as in sushi restaurants or in a packed lunchbox. You will need to purchase a square or rectangular pan, which is specifically designed for cooking *tamago yaki*. Although it takes some experience to perfect this dish, it is really quite simple with a little practice.

1 Heat the bonito stock, soy sauce, sugar, salt, and *mirin* in a saucepan over medium heat and remove from heat when it comes to a boil. Set aside to cool.
2 Add the cooled bonito stock mixture to the beaten eggs.
3 Heat a *tamago yaki* pan over medium heat and coat evenly with vegetable oil (see page 255).
4 Pour two ladles of the egg mixture into the pan. Tilt the pan so that the egg mixture is spread out evenly.
5 When the mixture begins to bubble, pierce the bubbles with chopsticks to remove the air.
6 When the mixture is about three-quarters cooked, slide the chopsticks under the cooked egg from the side furthest away from you and roll the egg towards you.
7 Slide the rolled egg back to the other side of the pan and coat the pan lightly with some more vegetable oil and pour another two ladles of the egg mixture into the pan and repeat steps 5 and 6 until the egg mixture is entirely cooked.
8 Cut the finished omelet into 6 pieces and serve hot with the grated radish.

Jellied citrus fruit

Yuzu gama warabi mochi

柚子釜わらびもち

Serves 4

5 *yuzu* (Japanese citron), although there
  is no substitute for this wonderful
  citrus, you may want to try using
  lemons for the casing, and a mixture
  of orange and lemon juice for the jelly
50 g *warabi ko* (bracken starch),
  substitute with *kuzu* (kudzu starch)
2/3 cup (130 g) superfine (castor) sugar
2 3/4 cups (700 ml) water
5 oz (150 g) palm sugar, ground with a
  knife, substitute with dark molasses
3/4 cup (200 ml) water
5 teaspoons plain syrup
1 tablespoon vinegar

Yuzu is a Japanese citrus with an extraordinary fragrant aroma. Normally only the zest is used, in slivers or grated, to spike soups and braised dishes but in the winter we use it for desserts or even float them in our soaking baths for their wonderful aroma, a kind of traditional aroma therapy.

1 Cut 4 of the *yuzu* across, about one-third from the top. Reserve the lids and spoon out the pulp to make 4 casings. Grate the zest of the fifth *yuzu*.
2 Place starch, superfine sugar, and 2 3/4 cups water in a saucepan and heat over medium heat, beating continuously with a whisk. When it reaches a boil, reduce the heat to low and cook for 20 minutes until the mixture becomes very thick. Stir continuously with a wooden spatula scraping the bottom of the saucepan to prevent it from catching. Remove from heat and cool.
3 When the mixture has cooled a little, add the grated citron zest.
4 Put the ground palm sugar, water, and syrup in a saucepan over low heat. When the sugar is completely melted, stir in the vinegar and remove from heat and cool.
5 Pour the cooled jelly mixture into the casings and chill. Pour the plam sugar mixture on the top of the jelly before serving. Cover the casings with their reserved lids.

Sticky rice cakes stuffed with sweet yam

Iimushi no imo an ikomi

飯蒸しの芋あん射込み

Serves 4
Dough
3 1/2 oz (100 g) *domyoji ko* (coarsely
   ground sticky rice powder)
Scant 1/2 cup (100 ml) lukewarm water,
   about 104°F (40°C)
2 1/2 teaspoons superfine (castor) sugar
Pinch natural sea salt

Purple sweet potato filling
5 oz (150 g) *kogane murasaki imo*
   (purple sweet potato), substitute with
   normal Japanese sweet potato or yams
1 tablespoon superfine (castor) sugar
Water
Lemon juice

Yellow potato filling
5 oz (150 g) *kogane satsuma imo*
   (orange sweet potato), substitute with
   normal Japanese sweet potato or yams
1 tablespoon superfine (castor) sugar
Water
Lemon juice

In the winter months, we sometimes use sweetened potato fillings instead of the usual sweet bean paste and we frequently use a purple sweet potato, *kogane murasaki imo*, for its exquisite color. If purple sweet potato is difficult to find, it can be substituted with normal yams or, perhaps for the color, with purple or truffle potatoes.

1 Put the rice powder in a bowl with the lukewarm water and leave for 30 minutes until the water is completely absorbed.
2 Keeping the purple and yellow sweet potatoes separate, slice them crosswise into 1/2-in (1-cm) thick slices. Peel the skin rather deeper than normal so that you remove the tougher part of the flesh. Steam the potato slices over medium high heat for 10 to 15 minutes until easily pierced with a skewer. Sieve or process the two batches separately into two lots of paste.
3 To make the fillings, put each potato paste into a small saucepan with the other ingredients over low heat and mix thoroughly with a wooden spatula, taking care that it does not scorch to the bottom of the pan. Cool and divide each batch into 6 portions. Set aside.
4 Mix the rice powder with the other dough ingredients gently so that you do not break the kernels. Steam in a bowl over medium heat for 5 minutes. Set aside until it is cool enough to handle then divide into 12 portions.
5 Spread each portion into a circle and place the potato filling in the center. Wrap the filling with the rice dough and gently form into a barrel shape. Serve immediately or reserve in a cool place, in a container covered with plastic wrap.

Apples baked in phyllo leaves

Ringo no filo zutsumi

りんごのフィロ包み

Serves 4
4 teaspoons unsalted butter
2 tart apples, peeled and cored, each
 cut vertically into 10 slices
1/4 cup (50 g) sugar
5 walnuts, sliced in half and toasted over
 medium heat until nicely browned
1/3 oz (10 g) raisins
8 phyllo sheets

Sauce
Scant 1/2 cup (100 g) sugar
1/2 cup (120 ml) water
1 tablespoon unsalted butter
2 tablespoons heavy (double) cream

This dessert is our version of apple strudel. Phyllo leaves are wonderful tissue-thin pastry sheets and extremely handy as they freeze well.

1 Preheat oven to 248°F (120°C, gas 1/2).
2 Melt the butter in a skillet and sauté the apple slices. Add the sugar and sauté until lightly browned. Remove from heat and add the walnuts and raisins.
3 Spread 2 phyllo leaves on a flat surface with edges slightly overlapping. Lightly grease with butter then place 2 slices of the sautéed apple with some walnuts and raisins at the right edge and roll towards the left. Repeat the process to make 4 rolls. Bake for 10 minutes.
4 Meanwhile, to make the sauce, combine the sugar and water in a saucepan and heat over high heat. When it begins to caramelize, add the butter and heavy cream at once. Mix vigorously and remove from heat.
5 Arrange the rolls on a plate, pour the sauce on top and garnish with the remaining 2 apple slices.

Baked fruit

Onsei furutsu

温製フルーツ

Serves 4
1 apple
3 1/4 cups (800 ml) water
Scant 1/2 cup (100 g) sugar
1/2 in (1 cm) vanilla bean
4 large or 8 small strawberries
1 teaspoon confectioners' (icing) sugar
4 dried persimmons
1 egg yolk, beaten together with a little
    water
1 teaspoon white sesame seeds

Custard sauce
1 egg yolk
3 2/3 cups (60 g) sugar
Scant 1/2 cup (100 ml) milk
4 tablespoons heavy (double) cream
1/2 in (1 cm) vanilla bean
2/3 oz (20 g) ogura an (sweet coarse
    azuki bean paste)
4 teaspoons (20 ml) water
2 stems of raisins

This is a warm baked fruit dessert for a chilly winter evening. In this recipe, we use *hoshi gaki*, or dried persimmon—a valuable preserved fruit for the long winter months. It can be found in Japanese grocery stores or you may try substituting dried apricots.

1 Preheat oven to 248°F (120°C, gas 1/2). Place the apple, water, sugar, and vanilla bean in a pan, cover and bake for 1 hour taking care not to burst the skin.
2 Increase oven temperature to 464°F (240°C, gas 9). Stand the strawberries upside down on a pie plate and sprinkle with confectioners' sugar. Bake in the oven to caramelize the sugar. When the sugar is lightly browned, remove the strawberries and repeat the process again until the sugar is caramelized.

3 Bake the dried persimmons, at the same temperature, for 10 minutes. Remove from oven and brush with the egg yolk mixture and sprinkle with white sesame seeds. Bake again until nicely browned.
4 To make the custard sauce, boil some water in a saucepan large enough to accommodate a bowl. Beat the egg yolk and sugar until lemon yellow, then add the milk, cream, and vanilla bean. Place the bowl in the saucepan of boiling water and beat with a whisk until thickened. Set aside.
5 Place the bean paste and water in a saucepan and heat over low heat until bubbling. Pour through a sieve to make a smooth sauce. Reserve and cool.
6 On a plate, arrange the strawberries and baked apple on a dollop of custard sauce and cover with sweet bean sauce. Place the baked dried persimmons on the same plate and garnish with raisins.

Waiting for dusk

Yoimachi

宵待ち

Makes 1 cocktail
4 teaspoons gin, chilled in the freezer
5 teaspoons *yuzu* (Japanese citron) liqueur
1 teaspoon fresh lime juice, strained of pulp
1 teaspoon fresh *yuzu* (Japanese citron) juice, substitute with bottled juice, or fresh lemon juice
Yuzu (Japanese citron) peel, sliced into thin slivers

This cocktail is made with *yuzu*, the extraordinary fragrant Japanese citrus which is used whole as a casing, its zest is used to spike soups or garnish dishes, and its juice used to make *ponzu* sauce. It is difficult to find outside of Japan in its fresh form but many Japanese grocery stores will carry its bottled juice. You can substitute lemon zest slivers for the garnish.

1 Shake all the ingredients together except for the *yuzu* peel.

2 Pour into a cocktail glass and garnish with slivers of *yuzu* peel.

appendices

- step by step preparation techniques
- glossary of ingredients
- mail-order sources of ingredients
- acknowledgments
- chefs

Three-section fillet

San mai oroshi
(For round fish, such as sea bream, sea bass, and striped jack.)

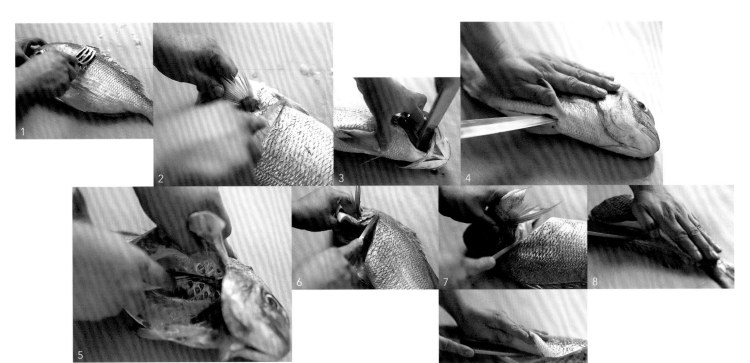

Cleaning *(mizu arai)*

1 Remove the scales with a fish scaler. Hold the fish by its head or tail so as not to bruise its flesh. An alternative is to use the base of the knife and run it from tail to head.

2 Lift the pectoral fin and remove the scales with the tip of your knife. It is very important to remove all the scales, as they will leave a fishy odor.

3 Insert the knife from under the gill flap, moving in a circular motion to cut the gill open. Lift the gill flap with your fingers and insert the knife into the throat, then cut the membrane connecting the inner gill to the collarbone, and turn the knife horizontally. Insert your fingers from under the jaw, and cut the inner gill out.

4 Cut lengthwise from the tail along the belly of the fish until the head. Remove the entrails. Cut out the bloodline that runs along the side of the backbone.

5 Clean out the inside of the fish with a whisk. Immediately wash the fish thoroughly to remove all traces of viscera, membrane, or blood.

6 Pat the fish dry and place on the cutting board with the head on your left, belly side closer to you. Cut along the line that joins the ventral and pelvic fin with your knife held at a slant. Stop at the depth when your knife hits the backbone.

7 Flip the fish over and repeat. Lift the fish by its head and insert the knife perpendicularly to extract the head from the joint connecting to the backbone. The head should be used for soup, grilled or braised.

Three-section fillet
(san mai oroshi)

8 Place the fish on the cutting board with the tail on the right, belly side closer to you. Insert the knife into the fish above the pelvic fin, keeping the cutting edge flat, and cut till the head.

9 Turn the fish around so that the tail is on your left; insert the knife into the fish above the dorsal fin, keeping the cutting edge flat; cut until the tail.

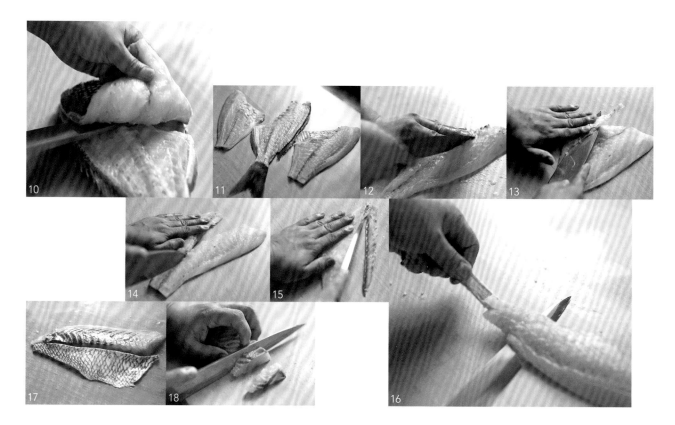

10 Lift the upper side of the fish and insert the knife with the blade flat. Cut with a sliding motion along the backbone towards the tail (do not cut any of the bones) until you have completely freed the top fillet all the way to the tail and the fish is cut into two sections. Flip the fish over and repeat on the bottom side.

11 Now you have three sections. Place the mid section (the section with bones) so that the fins hang over the edge of the cutting board, then cut the dorsal and ventral fins off. Save bones to make soup.

Removing the pelvic bone (*saku tori*)
12 Reverse the knife so that the blade is facing you. Use the tip of the knife to cut from bottom to top; lift up the edge of the pelvic bone to make a shallow cut.

13 With the knife in normal position, follow along the shallow cut and diagonally cut along the pelvic bone. At the edge, flip the pelvic bone over and sever.

14 Cut the top and bottom sections into lengthwise halves by cutting along the side of the blood line from head to tail. The two halved filleted sections are known as *saku*.

15 Remove any remaining trace of the blood line and ventral bone.

Skinning the fillets (*kawa no hiki kata*)
16 Place the belly and back sections on the cutting board, skin side down, head side to the right. Insert the knife with the blade flat between the skin and fillet. Slide the knife horizontally to the right while pulling the skin with your left hand.

17 You are now ready to cut the fillet using methods such as a brick cut (see step 18), or slant cut (see page 247).

Brick cut (*hira zukuri*)
18 Place the thicker side of *saku* away from you; insert the knife perpendicular to the thinner side and pull the knife towards you by snapping your wrist. Arrange on the dish perpendicularly. This is the most traditional cut of sashimi.

Five-section fillet

Go mai oroshi

(For flat fish, such as flounder.)

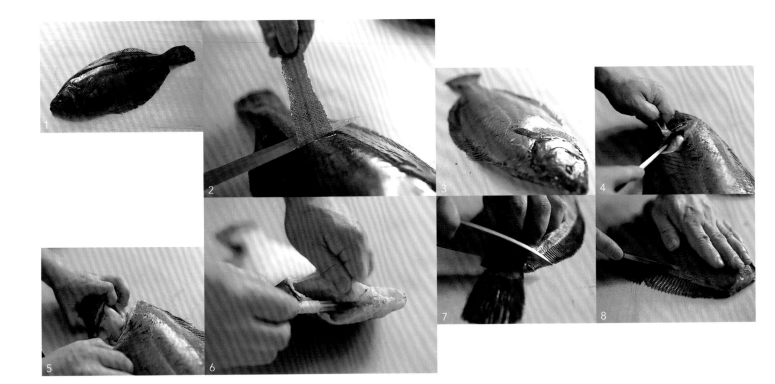

Cleaning (*mizu arai*)

1 Wash and place the fish on your cutting board.

2 With its head to your right, insert your knife horizontally at the base of the head and slide your knife between the scales and skin. Flip the fish over and remove the underside scales in the same manner.

3 The fish with all the scales removed. It is very important that you remove all the scales, as they will leave a fishy odor. Slant the fish to remove the scales around the fins.

4 Place the fish with the head to your left. Insert the tip of your knife and cut following the shape of the gill flap. Flip the fish over and cut in a V-shape.

5 Cut off the head. Pull out the head and the entrails

will come out together with the head.

6 Remove the red membrane with a whisk or bamboo skewers bunched together with a rubber band and wash thoroughly without delay. Pat dry and place on cutting board.

7 Cut the tail off.

Five-section fillet (*go mai oroshi*)

8 Place the fish on the cutting board with the head side closer to you. Insert the knife, with the blade flat, from the tail side into the side of the fish along the fins and cut with a sliding motion along the backbone towards the head, taking care not to cut any of the bones. This should be a shallow cut. You do not have to fillet the fish at this stage.

9 Insert the knife perpendicularly from the head side into the center of the fish until you hit the backbone and cut vertically along the ventral bone. Insert your knife horizontally with the blade flat from the head of the fish and slide the knife along the backbone. Cut horizontally along the backbone several times using the tip of your knife until you come to the previously made side cut to free the fillet from the backbone. Turn the fish around and insert your knife from the tail side of the backside and cut horizontally along the backbone several times using the tip of your knife to free the fillet from the backbone. Flip the fish over and repeat these steps for the underside of the fish.

10 Finished pieces from right to left: the underside belly section, the underside back section, the backbone, the topside back section, the topside belly section. (The edges of the fillets by the fins are referred to as *engawa* and are coveted sections for sashimi.)

11 Remove the pelvic bone by slicing diagonally.

12 Place the tail and back sections on the cutting board, skin side down, head side to the right. Insert the knife with the blade flat between the skin and fillet. Slide the knife horizontally to the right while pulling the skin with your left hand.

Slant cut (*sogi giri*)
13 Place the skinned side on top with the thicker side away from you. Hold the fish with your left hand, feeling the thickness of the slice you are making, and place the knife at a slant and pull the knife toward you. Lift each piece on the blade holding it with your left fore and middle fingers and arrange on the dish.

Bonito stock
Katsuo dashi (itten goban dashi)

Dashi stock is the basis of Japanese cuisine. The most common type of *dashi* is bonito stock which is made in two steps: *ichiban* (first) *dashi* and *niban* (second) *dashi*. *Ichiban dashi* is made by removing the dried bonito flakes immediately and, as such, is used for clear broth and glaze as it has a very delicate flavor and a tinge of color. *Niban dashi* is made by boiling the *konbu* and dried bonito flakes—which have already been used for making *ichiban dashi*—and is used in miso soups and for cooking as it has a stronger flavor and darker color. Any unused bonito flakes should be kept in the freezer for future use. Our *dashi* is in-between the *ichiban* and *niban dashi*, and is referred to as *itten goban dashi*.

1/2 oz (15 g) *dashi konbu* (dried kelp)
4 cups (2 liters) water
5 cups (50 g) dried bonito flakes, without bloodline

1 Gently wipe the sheet of *konbu* with a clean damp cloth or paper towel to remove the grit. The flavorful white powder on the surface should not be wiped off. Place *konbu* in a pot with the water.

2 Heat the water and *konbu* over medium-high heat. When the surface starts to foam, slightly lower the heat.

3 Just before the water reaches a full boil, remove *konbu* and reserve. Boiling *konbu* imparts a bitter flavor. Skim the foam off the surface with a ladle.

4 Add dried bonito flakes.

5 When the water starts to boil, lower the heat and maintain a wavering surface. Simmer for 5 or 6 minutes skimming the foam off the surface with a ladle.

6 Turn off the heat.

7 When the bonito flakes sink to the bottom, immediately strain in a sieve lined with *sarashi* (a kind of thin cotton cloth) or paper towel. The bonito stock is now ready for use.

Any remaining bonito flakes should be stored in the freezer for future use. The reserved *konbu* can be sliced finely into matchstick slivers and simmered in *tamari* soy sauce, *mirin*, and *sake* to make *tsukudani*, a salty-sweet condiment eaten with rice. Cool *tsukudani*, sprinkle with white sesame seeds and reserve in a non-reactive container. It will keep for about five days in the refrigerator.

Abalone
Awabi no shita goshirai

1 Remove the abalone from its shell by running a metal spatula or small knife between shell and meat; take care not to break the green liver.

2 Using the tip of your knife, insert into the mouth and cut it out in a V-shape.

3 Remove the green liver on the underside of the abalone. Reserve.

4 Place the abalone in a bowl and cover with a handful of sea salt.

5 Rub the salt in with your hands to remove any sliminess.

6 Scrub the abalone with a kitchen brush to further remove any sliminess and dark areas on the surface. Rinse the salt off by scrubbing with the kitchen brush in a bowl filled with water.

7 Trim the tough dark portion on the edge of the abalone. Pat dry.

Sushi rice and *nigiri* sushi

Sushi meshi to nigiri

1 Place the steaming hot rice in a *handai*, large wooden tub, or shallow wooden bowl. The wood absorbs the moisture from the steaming rice. Pour the vinegar mixture into the center of the rice.

2 Stir the rice gently with a wooden rice paddle or spatula to mix in the vinegar. Be careful not to bruise the soft rice grains. Using a horizontal motion, gently cut the vinegar into the rice with the rice paddle. While stirring the rice with one hand, use the other hand to fan the rice simultaneously. Fanning the rice is very important to evaporate the vinegar and to make the rice glossy. Continue for about 10 minutes. If the rice grains begin to stick to the paddle, dip in some water and continue stirring. Cover with damp cloth until ready for use. Do not refrigerate. Must be eaten the same day that it is made.

3 Prepare *nigiri* once all the other ingredients are prepared to prevent the rice from drying. Place about three tablespoons sushi rice on the palm of your left hand and press the top of the rice with your right forefinger and middle finger while pressing the sides by cradling it in your left palm to firm it into an oval shape.

4 Arrange any prepared ingredients on top of the *nigiri* sushi. Shown here is pickled *yamagobo* (wild burdock root), cut into 2-in (5-cm) lengths which is arranged on top of the *nigiri* sushi and tied with blanched *mitsuba* (trefoil).

Needle-thin vegetable slivers refreshed in water
Shiraganegi (sengiri) to sarasu

1 Shown here is *negi* (welsh onion) but the basic preparation is used for other similar vegetables. Cut into 2-in (5-cm) lengths. Make a vertical cut halfway until the core.

2 Remove the core.

3 Unroll the outer layers and flatten on the cutting board. Slice vertically into needle-thin slivers. This takes time and practice, and a well sharpened knife. Take time and cut diligently in straight and even motion.

4 Needle-thin slivers of *udo*, *myoga*, Japanese cucumber, carrot, and perilla are referred to as *sengiri*. Only *negi* slivers are referred to as *shiraga*.

5 Place slivers in a bowl of cold water. Refresh for 10 minutes, except for perilla which should only be refreshed, *sarasu*, very briefly so as not to lose its flavor.

Eggplant whisk cut
Nasu no chasen giri

1 Cut off the top of the eggplant. Make lengthwise incisions, about 2 mm apart and 1 1/4 in (3 cm) deep, all the way around the egg-plant, by turning the eggplant.

2 The incisions should resemble a whisk.

Butterfly-filleted, air-cured sweetfish

Ayu no sebiraki to ichiya boshi

1 Wash sweetfish thoroughly under running water to remove any sliminess and grit. Wipe gently with a paper towel.

2 Place on your cutting board lengthwise with the head away from you. Insert the tip of your knife, keeping the blade flat, from the tip of its head and cut along the dorsal fin making a shallow incision.

3 Continue to make the incision deeper until you can feel the backbone against your knife.

4 Continue the incision through the head to butter-fly cut the head. Remove the gills and entrails by running your blade lightly.

5 Wash the butterfly filleted fish in lightly salted water.

6 Dissolve 2 tablespoons natural sea salt in 4 cups water. Soak the filleted fish in the salt water for about 1 hour. Drain and place the filleted sweetfish, skin side down on a flat basket and air-cure overnight in a dry, cool place, preferably with some wind.

Fresh bamboo shoots
Takenoko no shita yude

1 Make certain that the shoot is very fresh, preferably dug up on the same day, and that it is still in its skin. Wash the shoot thoroughly under running water to remove any dirt. Cut off the top of the shoot about 1/5 of the way down at an angle. This allows for quicker cooking and releasing of the bitterness.

2 Make an incision lengthwise from the bottom of the shoot about 1/3 of the way up, about 1 1/4 to 2 in (3 to 5 cm) deep. Take care that you only cut through the layers of skin, and not the shoot itself. Slowly continue the incision for the remaining 2/3 of the shoot making a shallower cut, about 1/4 to 1/2 in (1/2 to 1 cm) deep.

3 In a large pot which can accommodate the shoots comfortably, place the shoots, 2/3 cup of *nuka* (rice bran), available at Japanese grocery stores, 2 or 3 dried red chili peppers and enough water to cover the shoots. Heat over high heat until it reaches boiling, then lower the heat to low and simmer for 1 to 2 hours depending on the size of the shoots, or until the bottom of the shoot can be easily pierced with a skewer. Remove from heat and let cool in the pot.

4 Wash the cooled bamboo shoot thoroughly under running water to remove all the rice bran. Gently open the incision with your hands and remove the layers of skin, leaving the thin layers of skin on the top of the shoot, about 1 in (2 to 3 cm).

5 Some of the thicker skin will remain on the shoot. You can remove that easily by running the dull side of your knife from the top of the shoot towards the bottom. Finally, wipe the bamboo shoot with a clean cloth so that it is thoroughly cleaned of any remaining skin and you can see its beautiful layering.

Note: Edible varieties of bamboo include *moso*, *nemagari*, *hachiku*, and *matake*.

Fresh soymilk
Tonyu no tsukuri kata

8 oz (250 g) dried soybeans
  (preferably organically
  grown)
6 cups (1 1/2 liters) water

1 Pour enough water over
the soybeans so that they
are covered. Soak the
soybeans: for 14 hours in
cold weather, or for 8 hours
in summer. The beans will
absorb the water and swell
to about double their size.

2 Pureé the beans in a food
processor. Process small
quantities at a time to
prevent the food processor
from over heating. Add

4 cups of water to the
puréed beans and process
for 5 minutes.

3 Check the coarseness of
the particles with your finger.
It may look creamy but it
should feel grainy. Process
for another 5 minutes and
the *go*, the raw material for
soymilk, is ready.

4 Heat the puréed soybean
mixture over low heat. Stir
continuously scraping the bottom of the pot with a wooden
spatula to prevent scorching.

5 Add 2 cups of boiling

water when the puréed
soybean mixture is warmed.

6 The surface should start
to foam like meringue. Stir
continuously for 15 to
20 minutes until the foam
subsides and settles to the
bottom of the pot.

7 Strain in a sieve lined with
sarashi (a kind of thin cotton) or cheesecloth large
enough to lift up and wring.

8 Use long chopsticks to hold
together the four corners of
the cloth and wring tightly.
Be careful, as it is extremely

hot. The residue left in the
cloth is known as *okara*.

9 Place soymilk into an
earthenware pot over low
heat, stirring with a wooden
or bamboo ladle scraping
the bottom to prevent from
scorching. When the tem-
perature reaches 167°F
(75°C)—normally in about
7 or 8 minutes—turn off the
heat. Pour in the bittern.

10 Stir the soymilk and
bittern with a wooden or
bamboo spoon.

11 Serve.

Fresh green bean soymilk yuba

Ryokuto nama yuba

1 Remove from heat once it reaches 176°F (80°C) and patiently wait until *yuba* forms on the surface. You can leave and check on the soymilk from time to time. Lift *yuba* out with chopsticks and soak in the reserved green soy milk. Make certain that all surfaces are coated to prevent from drying out. Heat the soymilk again and repeat this procedure until no more *yuba* forms. Discard remaining soymilk.

2 Chill *yuba* in the green soymilk, covered with plastic wrap or lid, this prevents it from drying out. Serve chilled with freshly grated wasabi and soy sauce. Refer to the recipe on page 54.

Japanese omelet

Tamago yaki no tsukuri kata

1 Heat a *tamago yaki* pan or other square or rectangular pan over medium heat and coat evenly with vegetable oil. Pour 2 ladles of egg mixture into the pan. Slide the pan around so that the egg mixture is spread out evenly.

2 When the mixture begins to bubble, pierce the bubbles with chopsticks to release air. When the mixture is about three-quarters cooked, slide the chopsticks under the cooked egg from the side furthest away from you and roll the egg towards you.

3 Slide the rolled egg back to the other side of the pan and coat the pan lightly with some more vegetable oil and pour another 2 ladles of egg mixture into the pan and repeat steps 1 through 3 until you have cooked the entire egg mixture.

4 The finished omelet. Refer to the recipe on page 232.

glossary

age deep-fried.

aka shiso perilla or beefsteak plant. Member of mint family and has a slightly basil-like flavor. It comes in two colors, red and green, used for coloring **umeboshi**.

an, ankake glazed sauce made with *kuzu* or **katakuri** and stock to thicken its consistency.

ao nori species of algae which grows on rocks by the ocean, photographed with **konbu**.

ayu sweetfish which lives only in the purest mountain streams. the coveted summer delicacy is edible whole as it only feeds on moss and has a very clean flavor compared to oyher river fish.

azuki *azuki* bean. A little red bean generally cooked whole with sugar or made into a paste, *an*, which is used as a filling for the majority of Japanese pastries. *Koshi an* is a smooth paste while *ogura an* has bits of bean. *An* is also cooked, unsweetened, with sticky rice to make *sekihan*.

bainiku sieved flesh of **umeboshi**, used as a dip or for sauce.

banno negi fine scallion (spring onion). The name literally means for all uses, and is used chopped finely as a condiment (photographed with **naga negi**).

beni imo wildly vivid purple sweet potato native to the tropical Okinawa Island.

beni tade water pepper, its tiny purple leaves with a peppery flavor are often served as a garnish for sashimi to be used with wasabi and soy sauce.

chasen bamboo whisk used for whipping *macha* (powdered green tea), but smaller ones are made for the purpose of brushing away the grated **yuzu** rind from the grater.

chirimen jako see **jako**.

chomiryo seasonings such as natural sea salt, **shoyu** (soy sauce), **mirin** (sweet cooking sake), **miso**, and **su** (vinegar). Seasonings and sauces are key ingredients in creating a successful dish.

daikon giant white radish. An important vegetable in Japanese cuisine for **nimono** (braised dishes) or grated to be used with soy sauce for **sashimi** or **tempura** dipping sauce because it is known to be digestive for oily foods

domyoji ko see **mochi gome**

edamame young green soybean in the pod. Boiled on the stalk with sea salt, they are a typical summer side dish served with beer.

endomame green peas. Spring ingredient for rice, puréed cold soup, and tofu.

enoki dake *enoki* mushroom. Clusters of tiny white mushrooms with thin long stalks.

fugu negi very thin, green scallion (spring onion), most commonly used finely chopped as a condiment for *fugu* (blowfish). (Photographed with **shimonita negi**).

fuki Japanese butterbur that resembles a rhubarb, a stalk spring vegetable reminiscent of celery.

fuki no to unopened bud of butterbur, refer to **sansai**.

gobo burdock root, rich in dietary fiber and vitamins; it should always be soaked in cold water with vinegar added to remove its bitterness.

goma sesame seeds, *shiro* (white) or *kuro* (black), should be toasted in a dry pan before using to give off a pungent aroma (photographed with **neri goma**, a paste made from white sesame).

hakusai Chinese cabbage

hakuto white peach, varieties called *Shimizu Hakuto* widely cultivated in Okayama Prefecture, and Hakuho, from Yamanashi Prefecture, are the most coveted for its high water and sugar content.

hana hojiso flower buds of *shiso* plant, used as garnish for **sashimi**, refer to **shiso**.

hanshi Japanese paper originally used as writing paper, but as it absorbs oil, it is placed under deep-fried foods. Sometimes it is referred to as *tenshi* because *hanshi* is most commonly used for **tempura**.

harusame spring rain noodles, cellophane noodles or mung bean vermicelli.

hojiso leaf buds of **shiso** plant, used as condiment for **sashimi**, refer to **shiso**.

ingen snap bean

ito gaki extra thin *bonito* shavings, literally translated as thread.

jako tiny baby sardines or anchovies (*shirasu*), which are boiled and air cured.

joshinko non-glutinous rice flour

junsai shoots of water shield, a lotus-like water plant. The shoots come out in early summer, have a gelatinous coating, and are very slippery. They have no flavor but are coveted for its gelatinous texture. Most often used in *sunomono* (vinegared dish) with *sanbaizu* or *suimono* (clear soup).

kabu turnip. Harvested in autumn and winter, appearing in various sizes and colors, and much more tender and white than the Western turnip, *kabu* root is used for **nimono** (braised dishes) or *tsukemono* (pickles). The leaves are also delicious and used for *tsukemono* (pickles). Also shown: the large round *kyo kabu* or *shogoin kabura* from Kyoto, famous for *senmaizuke* (Kyoto pickle) or *kaburamushi* (grated and steamed turnip).

kaki persimmon. An autumn fruit which comes in two varieties, *amagaki* (sweet) and *shibugaki* (astringent). The popular varieties of the sweet are *Nishimura Awase* and *Zenjimaru*, and the popular varieties of astringent are *Hiratanenashi* and *Koshu Hyakume* are often dried and eaten in the winter.

kaki age fritter, a kind of **tempura**, chopped vegetables or small shellfish is batter fried together in clumps.

kanpyo dried gourd strips. It is most familiar braised and used as a filling for *maki zushi*, laver rolled sushi, but is also used as an edible tying string.

kanten agar-agar, made from red algae used like gelatin to make jellied dishes—difficult to substitute with gelatin since it produces a much firmer texture.

kara age deep-fried, ingredients are deep-fried without any coating or with seasoned flour.

katakuri thickening starch originally made from Japanese violet, but because this violet is so scarce and expensive now, potato starch is more commonly known by the same name.

katsuo bushi dried, mold-cured bonito fillet. The bonito fillet is boiled, dried, then smoked and finally cured with a mold to create an extremely hard wood-like substance. It is shaved to be used for making *dashi* broth or as a garnish and condiment. As with **konbu** it is considered to be one of the most essential ingredients in Japanese cuisine.

kawa nori a species of algae which grows on rocks in cold mountain streams.

kezuribushi shaved **katsuo bushi** flakes

kinome young leaves of **sansho** tree, prickly Japanese ash.

kobu cha powdered kelp, to be dissolved with hot water to make a kind of tea, although no tea leaves are actually in the powder.

kochujang korean red chili pepper paste.

kogane satsuma imo a variety of orange sweet potato

kogomi fiddlehead of ostrich fern, refer to **sansai**

koikuchi shoyu dark soy sauce, refer to **shoyu**

koji miso refer to **miso**

ko nasu photographed with *mizu nasu*, miniature eggplant, *Minden* from Tohoku (northern Japan) and *Mogi* from Kyoto are famous.

konbu shown here with **nori** and **wakame**. One of the most essential ingredients in Japanese cuisine, as it is used in making the basic *dashi* broth. **Konbu** grows in cold waters off the coasts of northern Japan, Rishiri *konbu* and Rause *konbu* harvested in Hokkaido are the most coveted. The dried blades can be in lengths up to 1 meter. Used *konbu* (after making *dashi* broth) can be cut into thin slivers and braised in soy sauce,

mirin and sugar to make *tsuku-dani*, a condiment eaten with rice.

Korean red pepper flakes There are a great variety of dried red chili peppers in Korea; the large flakes are much sweeter in flavor and more brilliant in color than the very hot Japanese red pepper flakes made from a smaller variety of red chili pepper. Store in the refrigerator. Photographed together are: **Korean red pepper threads**, fine slivers of Korean dried red chili peppers (bottom left), **taka no tsume** whole dried red chili peppers (bottom right), **yuzu togarashi** spicy paste made from **yuzu** and dried red chili pepper in Saga Prefecture (top right).

Korean virgin sesame oil a wonderfully aromatic and light sesame oil made by Pulmuone Company (organic food manufacturer in Korea). This sesame oil should be used for drizzling as a seasoning, not as a cooking oil.

kyoho a variety of grape developed in Japan and introduced in 1945, widely harvested in Yamanashi Prefecture, is an extremely expensive and coveted fruit.

kyo kabu refer to **kabu** and **shogoin kabura**, photographed with *kabu*.

kyo ninjin a carrot from Kyoto that has a much stronger flavor and color than the normal variety mainly used for braised dishes.

kyuri cucumber. The Japanese cucumber is very thin and without the large seeds found in Western cucumbers. Can be substituted with an English cucumber.

maitake hen-of-the-woods fungus, a very fragrant autumn fungus which is widely cultivated.

matsutake pine mushroom. One of the most coveted and expensive delicacies in Japanese cuisine. It is a wild fungus which grows in sandy dirt in red pine forests, and are extremely difficult to find. The most famous are from Tamba (the mountainous region of Kyoto) with a highly aromatic flavor and unique texture. There is even a specialty store in Kyoto which only opens for two months out of a year to sell the precious fungus. Because the domestic fungus is extremely expensive and becoming very scarce, they are imported on a very large scale from Korea, China and Canada. Harvested in autumn, can be charcoal grilled whole, cooked in rice or served in *dobinmushi* (soup). It is always served with **sudachi**.

menegi sprouts of *kujo negi* (welsh onion or *chibol*), native to Kyoto.

mentaiko spicy cod roe

mibuna a green leafy vegetable from Kyoto which is harvested in winter, used for **nabe** and **nimono**.

mirin sweet cooking *sake* photograhed with **su**. Our Kokonoe Sakura *mirin* dating back to 1772, from Aichi Prefecture, is made

from steamed organically grown rice which is fermented with a mold. It is then distilled for 60 days. It has an alcohol content of about 14%. Used exclusively for cooking and cannot be drunk or substituted with the beverage *sake*.

miso a fermented paste of soybeans, barley or rice and salt. It is highly nutritious, having 14% protein, and is very tasty, with almost a meat-like flavor. It was originally developed in Mongolia and arrived to Japan through the Korean peninsula. **red miso** (aka **miso**) is the most popular and widely used amongst all the different varieties. It is normally made with rice and is reddish brown in color. As it is quite salty, it is often mixed with white miso as *awase* miso when it is used for soup. Our Izutsu miso is made in Kagawa Prefecture with organically grown soybeans **white miso** (*shiro* miso) is normally not used on its own except in Western Japan where *saikyo* miso, especially in Kyoto, is popular. It is quite sweet and very different from the normal . salty variety. It is used for soups in Western Japan and for marinating fish. **Hatcho miso** is a very dark miso made strictly with soybeans and it is favored in central Japan.The soups served in higher-class establishments will often serve *akadashi* that is made with this miso. Our Kakukyu miso is made with organically grown soybeans. **Koji miso** is a kind of red miso made with a higher percentage of rice, making it less salty.

moromi miso chopped vegetables are added to the fermentation process and the outcome is a softer and milder miso; it is often eaten with cucumber sticks.

mitsuba trefoil, Japanese wild chervil. A popular herb used in soups, vinegared foods and as a garnish. Its name is literally translated as "three leaves" and is similar looking to Italian parsley or coriander but its taste is more similar to a mild chervil.

mizu konro charcoal brazier, double layered, one layer used to house the lit charcoal and the outside cover should be filled with water to collect the hot ashes.

mizuna a green leaf vegetable from Kyoto which is harvested in winter, used for **nabe** and **nimono**.

mizu nasu photographed with **ko nasu**, a type of eggplant from Senshu, Osaka-fu, highly prized for *asazuke* (slightly pickled) because of its rich water content and is served whole to be shredded by your fingers.

mochi sticky rice cake, which is pounded from steamed glutinous rice.

mochi gome glutinous rice normally used to make *mochi* or

the various powders used for making Japanese confections.

domyoji ko a roughly ground powder made from steamed glutinous rice, used to make a confection called *ohagi*.

mochi ko a finely ground powder from uncooked glutinous rice, for making *daifuku*, a confection.

shiratama ko, a finely ground powder from uncooked but water soaked glutinous rice, used to make a confection called *shiratama* or *daifuku*.

mura me tiny young leaves of red **shiso** served as a garnish for **sashimi** to be used with **wasabi** and soy sauce.

myoga *myoga* or ginger buds, harvested in the rainy season months of summer, cut into *sengiri* and used in salads, *shiomomi* and garnish for **sashimi** or pickled whole in sweetened **su** (vinegar).

nabe pot; hot pot meal

naga imo Japanese yam, photographed with **yama imo**.

Japanese yams come in great variety of shapes, long, round or glove shaped. Originally harvested in the autumn, the wild long variety is known as **jinenjo**, they are cultivated all year in most parts of Japan. *Naga imo* contains more water than the others and is delicious eaten raw in salads. The other varieties are grated and become very slippery. Can be eaten raw in the grated form, mixed with *katsuo dashi* and soy sauce to be served over hot rice cooked with wheat, or mixed in with other ingredients and cooked.

naga negi welsh onion, Japanese bunching onion or *chibol*. This is the most common of the *negi* family and is used in braised dishes, *nabe* dishes, and finely sliced as a condiment as in *sarashi negi*.

nagashigata a square or rectangular metal mold with an insert for easy removal, used for molding jellied dishes.

nano hana rape shoots, one of the favorite "coming of spring" vegetables.

nashi Japanese pear, often referred to as pear apple since it has a pear-like flavor and apple like crispness. There are brown, *Kosui* and *Niitaka*, and yellow *Nijuseiki*, varieties.

nasu eggplant, much smaller in size and less bitter than the Western eggplant, used for *tsukemono*, **tempura**, and *shiomomi*.

natural sea salt Our natural sea salt is from Izu Oshima Island and from Itoman, Okinawa Prefecture, and is made employing centuries-old methods. The salt water is spread on the salt fields, where the water is evaporated by the strong ocean sun. This salt is then harvested and broiled on large slats for final drying. This salt has a wonderful bittersweet flavor and is rich in natural minerals contained in the ocean such as calcium, magnesium, and nitrate.

neri goma sesame paste (photographed with **goma**), white sesame seeds are toasted to golden brown and pulverized until it becomes a creamy paste like peanut butter.

ni braised

nimono braised dish

nigari bittern, residue of sea salt (magnesium chloride) used as a coagulant for tofu.

nobiru red garlic, refer to **sansai**.

nori laver, dried sheets of algae, photographed with **konbu** and *wakame*. Originally collected at low tide but it has been cultivated along most of the coasts of Japan except for Hokkaido since the Edo period. The better known is *asakusa nori* which is made from a red algae. The large sheets of *nori* (22 cm by 17 cm) should be toasted, by holding it above a grill over a low flame and turning it over, just before eating and cut into small rectangular squares. You pick up bite-sized morsels of rice with your chopsticks and wrap with *nori*. Although nowadays, you will find pre-toasted and pre-cut *nori*. There is also *iwa nori* or *ao nori* which is a different species of algae that grows on rocks by the ocean and *kawa nori* which grows on rocks in cold mountain streams.

nuka rice bran, mixed into a soft paste with water, salt and dried red chili peppers as a picking medium, *nukazuke*.

ogura an refer to **azuki**

okara tofu lees, the bran residue of soybean left in the process of making the soymilk for making tofu.

ponzu the juice of Japanese citrus, although more commonly known as a dipping sauce made from a mixture of *sake*, alcohol burned off, soy sauce and this citrus juice squeezed from *daidai*, *kabosu*, *sudachi* and sometimes *yuzu*.

renkon lotus root

rice short grain rice, Japonica species. Although often referred to as glutinous or sticky rice, the rice most commonly eaten by the Japanese, *uruchi mai*, is non-glutinous. (The glutinous variety is known as **mochi gome**.) It can be found in most supermarkets now, mostly produced in California, the organic Japanese rice from the Lundberg farms is very good as well as Nishiki from JFC International. Many Japanese rice packages say that it is not necessary to wash but Japanese rice is polished and coated with fine talc which must be washed off. Wash the rice thoroughly until the water runs clear at least one hour before using, soak in water for 30 minutes, drain and let stand for another 30 minutes before cooking. Place the rice in a heavy lidded pot and add the measured water. Bring to a full boil over high heat uncovered. Lower the heat to low, cover and cook for 30 minutes. Remove from heat and let stand for 10 minutes. Fluff with a wooden spatula and serve.

sake rice wine, although strictly speaking this is not a wine since it is made from a grain. The two most important ingredients for making good *sake* are rice and water. Therefore the most prestigious *sake* brewers exist in regions where high quality rice is cultivated with an abundant supply of pure spring water. *Sake* is made by fermenting steamed polished rice with *koji* (molded steamed rice) and yeast with pure spring water. The *koji* converts the starch content in the rice to sugar and the yeast starts the alcohol fermentation which is continued for three months. The best *sake* is made in the cold winter months and called *kanzukuri*. The fermented mixture is then pressed through a cloth and filtered or left to settle into a transparent state. The polishing of the rice is also an important factor in determining the rank of the *sake*. All *sake* with the exception of *honjozo* should be refrigerated, and should be consumed within three months. *Sake* does not age well like wine.
ginjo *Ginjo sake* is brewed from rice, which has been polished down to 60% or less.
daiginjo *Daiginjo sake* is brewed from rice that has been polished down to 50% or less.
junmai Pure *sake*, *junmai sake* is brewed from rice and malted

rice only, no alcohol is added.
honjozo *Honjozo* is *sake* to which a limited amount of brewer's alcohol has been added. Suited for serving hot.
yamahai ginjo Literally translated as "without the *yamaoroshi* process that was a method of pulverizing the rice to quickly make the mold for fermenting the *sake* many years ago". This has been replaced by a more efficient method in recent years.

sakura no hana no shio zuke salt preserved cherry blossoms, often used to make a hot drink served at celebrations such as weddings.

san-go-hachi pickling medium from Aizu (Fukushima Prefecture) made from 3 parts salt, 5 parts *koji* (malted rice), and 8 parts rice.

sansai mountain vegetable. Spring favorite although some *sansai* is eaten in the autumn. Many varieties of *sansai* are now cultivated but there is no comparison to the wild originals picked from the mountains. They have a distinctive bitter flavor and time is of essence, otherwise they oxidize and become very bitter. Listed below are some of the varieties.
fuki no to unopened bud of butterburs

kogomi fiddlehead of ostrich fern
nobiru red garlic
taranome shoot of angelica tree
udo a stalk plant similar in texture and fragrance to celery
urui shoot of hosta plant

sarasu to refresh in cold water

sashimi sliced raw fish

sato imo Japanese taro potato

satsuma imo sweet potato

seri water dropwort, reminiscent of watercress in appearance and taste, is a wild spring vegetable growing in streams and marshes.

sengiri sliced into needle thin slivers

shiitake *shiitake* mushroom, best known out of the Japanese fungus, used fresh or dried and reconstituted. It takes its name after *shii* tree (kind of oak) since it is cultivated on *shii* logs and harvested in the spring and autumn. The most coveted are *donko* (cap is thick and curled under). Used for charcoal grilling, *tempura*, *nabe*, and *nimono*.

shimeji *shimeji* mushroom, clusters of small straw-colored mushrooms.

shimonita negi a thick welsh onion or *chibol* resembling the western leek, photographed with **fugu negi**. It is cultivated in Shimonita Village in Gunma Prefecture and is used for charcoal grilling or **nimono** rather than a condiment as the other members of **negi** family since it is much thicker in diameter and has a softer texture.

shiomomi salt pressed, simplest form of pickles made by hand pressing thinly sliced vegetables with natural sea salt.

shiraga negi needle thin slivers of *negi* (**sengiri**), often refreshed in cold water (**sarashi**), typical garnish and condiment.

shiratama ko refer to **mochi gome**

shiro soy sauce white soy sauce, almost transparent in color, refer to **shoyu**.

shiro uri Asian pickling melon

shiso perilla or beefsteak plant. Member of mint family and has a slightly basil-like flavor. It comes in two colors, **aka shiso** (red), used for making *umeboshi* (salt pickled plum) and *shiso* (green), sliced into **sengiri** is used as a condiment or whole as a garnish. The flower buds (*hana hojiso*) are used for garnish and very young left buds on the stalk (*ho jiso*) are pickled. If you are planning to cook many Japanese dishes, it is very east to cultivate *shiso* plant in a pot like basil plant. You can harvest the leaves, buds and flowers.

shogoin kabura also known as *kyo kabu*, this is a giant turnip from Kyoto which was named after the area in which it was cultivated in 1716, refer to **kabu**.

shoyu soy sauce
koikuchi shoyu is the most widely used soy sauce. Often referred to as dark, in comparison to the pale soy sauce, it is however the standard soy sauce, not to be confused with tamari soy sauce, which is dark and heavy. The Marushima soy sauce is from Uchinomi Village on Shodo Island, Kagawa Prefecture and is made from the highest quality soybean, organically grown wheat, natural rock salt and pure spring water from the Reihokankake Mountain, and is brewed in the ancient method using wooden barrels. The shoyu is barreled for a minimum

of three years and is rich in protein, calcium, and iron. It has a very mild sweetness in comparison to other soy sauces, which are simply salty.
usukuchi shoyu is a pale soy sauce, used when you do not want to discolor food material or sauce, and originally from Kyoto. It is somewhat saltier than the standard *koikuchi* and should be used with caution. The lighter color is a result of shorter periods of maturation and higher salt content. The *Genmyo* soy sauce is brewed in the ancient method using wooden barrels in Niigata Prefecture.
shiro shoyu white soy sauce, almost transparent in color. The *Marugo* soy sauce is made in Hiroshima Prefecture from milled wheat and soybean. The soybean content is very low and therefore its taste is very simple in comparison to the other soy sauces. Used for dishes where you do not want to color the ingredients or soup.
tamari shoyu dark, heavy soy sauce. Unlike the other soy sauces, it is brewed with virtually no wheat and is mostly made in Aichi, Mie, and Gifu Prefectures. It is mainly used for **sashimi** dipping sauce and for broiling sauce, which requires a darker and stronger flavor. Our Sekigahara soy sauce is made in Gifu Prefecture and this is the officially appointed tamari for use in the Imperial Palace.

shungiku chrysanthemum leaves

soramame broad bean, fava bean. Grilled in the pod or boiled with sea salt, they are a typical spring side dish. Spring ingredient for pureed cold soup and tofu.

su rice vinegar, low in acidity about 4.2%, photographed with mirin. Our Chidori Vinegar has been made for over 270 years by fermenting organically grown young rice, and distilled and matured in wooden barrels in Kyoto.

sudachi Japanese citrus with a sharp acidic flavor, a must accompaniment for **matsutake** and some **sashimi** dishes, used in its green unripened state.

suribachi ribbed earthenware mortar, used commonly for grinding sesame with a wooden pestle called *surikogi*.

sushi raw fish served on vinegared rice. There is no question that sushi is the most internationally acclaimed Japanese dish. In reality, *sushi* in the form that it is recognized internationally is called *edomae*. It was originally developed in the Edo (original name for Tokyo) period from 1600 to 1800 when the name Tokyo was adopted with start of the Meiji Era.

tade willow-like herb, normally steeped in vinegar to be used as a dipping sauce for **ayu**.

takana mustard green, originally from China, most often pickled in salt in Northern Japan for the long, cold winter months.

taka no tsume literally translated as hawk's claw as it resembles its shape, dried variety of extremely hot red chili pepper, there are Japanese and Chinese varieties, photographed with Korean red pepper flakes.

takenoko bamboo shoot. A spring delicacy, the most popular shoot is from *mosodake* (species of bamboo), and occasionally from *madake*. A much thinner variety such as *himedake* and *hachiku* is eaten in late spring. The thick *mosodake* variety is first boiled with **nuka** and red chili pepper to remove its bitterness before using to prepare dishes, but the most delicious and indulgent way to savor the bamboo shoot is to charcoal broil immediately after being dug out at when it has not yet oxidized and become bitter.

tamari shoyu dark soy sauce, refer to **shoyu**.

taranome shoot of angelica tree, refer to **sansai**.

tempura batter fried seafood and vegetables

toban djan Chinese fava bean and red chili pepper paste.

tofu bean curd

togan gourd, originally from Southeast Asia

tsukune imo Japanese yam from Kyoto, photographed with **kyo imo**.

udo asparagus like stalk plant Wild *udo* belongs to the *sansai* grouping and is a spring favorite. Cultivated *udo* is more often available these days and is white in color since it is grown in the dark and has a more restrained flavor.

udon wheat noodles, available in fresh or dried form

ume Japanese apricot, generally translated as Japanese plum but in reality it is a kind of apricot *Nanko* from Wakayama Prefecture, harvested in mid to late June, is the most coveted because of its rich flavor and large size.

umeboshi dried, salt pickled **ume**, colored with red **shiso** leaves. A traditional saying goes that one should eat three *ume-boshi* each morning for health. It is eye-opener, digestive stimulant, and hangover cure. We only use *umeboshi* made with the prized *Nanko ume*. It is generally eaten as a pickled for breakfast or for packed lunches, bento, but we use it to make *bainiku* or to season soups.

umeshu Japanese apricot liquor, generally translated as plum wine, *ume* macerated in *shochu*, a vodka-like spirit made from rice, barley, potato or sesame, and rock sugar. Can be store bought, but we, like some families

continue the tradition, make our own. The flavor mellows significantly with age.

urui shoot of hosta plant, refer to **sansai**

usukuchi soy sauce, refer to **shoyu**

wagarashi ko powdered Japanese mustard, hotter than English mustard, used as a condiment, in dressing or for pickling medium for mustard *tsukemono*.

wakame seaweed, photographed with **konbu** and **nori**. It is harvested in Hokkaido, Sanriku and Sea of Japan, and is best when it is fresh, but can now be bought dried or salt preserved and reconstitutes very quickly in water. Normally used in *miso* soup, dressed with vinegared sauce in *aemono*, or as a garnish for **sashimi**.

wakegi refer to **negi**

wasabi originally grows wild and only in cool and shaded mountain streams but is recently cultivated on the banks of streams or idle rice fields. Fresh wasabi is expensive and its presence distinguishes the class of the establishment. The entire root can be grated and should be grated downward beginning at just below the leaf stalks. The best grater to use is the skin of *korosame* (angel shark), attached to a piece of wood but of course, metal graters can be substituted.

yaki broiled

yamagobo wild burdock root, cultivated nowadays in Nagano and Aichi Prefectures, often eaten as a pickle, pickled in miso or soy sauce.

yamato imo Japanese yam, photographed with **naga imo**.

yuba famous as a Kyoto delicacy, it is the film which forms on the surface when soy milk is heated, similar to the film which forms on the surface of heated milk. As it absorbs the majority of the protein contained in soy milk, it is the richest source of protein known to exist. Nearly all fresh *yuba* is produced in Kyoto and is very expensive because of the time consuming handwork and refrigerated transportation costs, as it must be served very fresh.

yubiki blanched

yuzu Japanese citrus with an extraordinary fragrant aroma Normally only the zest is used, in slivers or grated, to spike soups and braised dishes. The remaining fruit can be squeezed to make *yuzu* **ponzu** although *ponzu* is normally made from *daidai* or *kabosu*.

yuzu togarashi spicy paste made from **yuzu** and dried red chili pepper in Saga Prefecture, photographed with **Korean red pepper flakes**.

zosui a rice gruel cooked with soup, normally in the soup left at the end of your **nabe**.

mail-order sources of ingredients

The majority of ingredients used in this book can be found in markets featuring the foods of Japan and East Asia. Many of them can also be found in any well-stocked supermarket. Ingredients not found locally may be available from the mail-order markets listed below.

USA
Maruwa.com
1746 Post St, San Francisco, CA 94115, USA
Tel 1 415 771 2583
Fax 1 415 771 7356
www.maruwa.com
info@maruwa.com

Diamond Organics,
PO Box 2159, Freedom, CA 95019, USA
Tel 1 888 674 2642
Fax 1 888 888 6777
www.diamondorganics.com
info@diamondorganics.com

Umpqua Organic Farm
Roseburg, Oregon, USA
Tel 1 541 673 3223
www.asianpearsorganic.com

Frog Hollow Farm
PO Box 872, Brentwood, CA 94513, USA
Tel 1 888 779 4511
Fax 1 925 516 2332
peaches@froghollow.com
www.froghollow.com
Pacific Farms USA LP
88420 Highway 101 N.,

Florence, OR 97430, USA
Tel 1 800 927 2248
info@freshwasabi.com
www.freshwasabi.com

Sushi Foods Co.
Tel 1 888 817 8744
Fax 1 619 222 0865
info@sushifoods.com
www.sushifoods.com

Quickspice.com
(near port of Los Angeles)
Tel 1 800 553 5008
Fax 1 323 464 7713
comments@quickspice.com
www.quickspice.com

eSake USA
Tel 1 415 398 9463
Fax 1 415 981 9132
salesUSA@esake.com
www.esake.com

eSake Japan
3-12-1 Moriminami
Katano-shi Osaka 576-0031
Japan
Tel 81 0467 24 2384
Fax 81 072 891 0354
sales@esake.com

UK
Mount Fuji International
Felton Butler, Shrewsbury
SY4 1AS, UK
Tel 01743 741 169
Fax 01743 741 650
sales@mountfuji.co.uk
www.mountfuji.co.uk

acknowledgments

Following is a list of our contributing artists, kilns, and producers whose works are photographed in this book.

Yoko Akino
Aritsugu
Ryo Aoki
Satoshi Aoki
Michihiko Arai
Doraku
Noriyuki Fujii
Noa Hanyu
Kiyoshi Hara
Tadashi Ito
Tadashi Kakamu

Tsubusa Kato
Taizo Kuroda
Touru Matsuzaki
Mino Seizan, Inc.
Shigeyoshi Morioka
Yuri Morioka
Takashi Nakazato
Yoshihisa Okuda
Toyoki Ooshima
Soho Sagawa
Yoshihiko Takahashi
Shinya Totani
Seimei Tsuji
Hiroyuki Yoshitoshi

We would like to thank Toshiaki Hirai of Super Potato for unwavering support of every detailed step to completion.

Yaeko Masuda of Jungle and Horizon for her unfailing energy and spirit boosting during our treacherous all-night shootings.

Mitsuo Yamazaki and his family for their never ending cooperation with our summer and autumn location shootings.

Katahira family for their generous hospitality during our bamboo shoot harvest.

Norihisa Usui of Seikosha for his support with shootings.

Ichiro Hirose of Tokyo Gallery for his generous loan of dishware.

Reiko Okamoto for her ideas and support.

And mostly, to each and every one of our staff at Shunju.

chefs

A veteran of the industry with almost 30 years' experience, **Toshimi Yamasaki**, began his career in Japanese, French, and Chinese cuisine, before joining Shunju at Mishuku as Chef. After a promotion to Chef/Manager at Mishuku, Yamasaki was later appointed Executive Chef at the Shunju headquarters.

Yuji Tomizawa began his career in Italian cuisine, which includes experience at the Bice Restaurant in the Four Seasons Hotel in Tokyo. Tomizawa joined Shunju at Toriizaka. He was subsequently Second Chef at Shunju in Bunkamura-dori after which he was recently promoted to Chef.

A graduate of Moranbon Culinary Institute, **Tokisaburo Asamizu** boasts 25 years' experience in Japanese, French, Swiss, and other western cuisine. Asamizu joined Shunju at Mishuku where he was appointed Second Chef. He was subsequently appointed Chef at Shunju in Hiroo and more recently at Toriizaka.

Kaoru Shiba graduated from the Seishin Culinary Institute and has over 25 years' experience in Japanese, French, and other western cuisine. Shiba started with Shunju as Second Chef at Mishuku, and was later promoted to Chef. Yet later he was appointed Chef at Tameike Sanno.

A graduate of Shinjuku Culinary Institute, **Shoji Yanase** began his career in French cuisine, and also spent a year in Toulouse, France. Yanase joined Shunju at Hiroo where he was appointed Second Chef. He was subsequently appointed Chef at Shunju in Bunkamura dori and more recently at Hiroo.

Yoshikazu Handa's experience includes a stint as Chef at the Japanese Embassy in Bulgaria, and as a student in Taillevent, Paris, France. With a background in French cuisine, Handa joined Shunju at Hiroo where he was appointed Second Chef, and then Chef. He was later Chef at Tameike Sanno before he subsequently opened his own restaurant.

index

In memory of Katsuya Wada
1955 – 1999